COMING HOME TO THE HEART

COMING HOME
TO THE HEART

TRANSFORMING TRAUMA INTO
INFINITE POSSIBILITIES FOR HEALING

RICHA BADAMI

Richa Badami, Inc.
42020 Village Center Plaza
Suite 120-135
Stone Ridge, VA 20105
USA

ISBN: 978-0-9969562-0-8

Design and typesetting: Bellerophon Productions

Front cover photo: Charles Martin

Copyeditor: Kathy Hollen

Proofreader: Bob Land

Printed by Createspace

Richa Badami, Inc.
42020 Village Center Plaza
Suite 120-135
Stone Ridge, VA 20105
USA

Website: www.RichaBadami.com
Email: Richa@RichaBadami.com

Dedication

I dedicate this book to all those who have suffered the trauma of child-hood abuse, molestation, or incest as well as to those who have been compelled to inflict it. Further, I dedicate it to victims' husbands, wives, partners, lovers, siblings, parents, and children.

Table of Contents

Preface

Is it possible to completely heal from psychological trauma? The simple answer is yes. Yes, it is, and this means it's possible to live your life to your fullest potential, released from negative patterns and limiting beliefs. You *can* heal, you *can* speak your truth, you *can* align with your higher purpose, you *can* tap into your inner power and fully inhabit the life you were born to live.

How do you heal from a hurtful past? How do you learn to see yourself as someone who is whole and worthy of love and respect after deep wounds? How do you begin to love the person you are when you have spent so many years in the dark recesses of your mind doing the opposite?

Recovering from a traumatic past, whether from abuse, divorce, financial ruin, or the loss of a loved one, is like taking a journey in your car. And, just as you would during any journey, you will encounter stoplights, right and left turns, detours, and even U-turns. Sometimes you'll be cruising along and your car will break down, possibly requiring maintenance. Sometimes it might run out of gas. Sometimes you might give someone a lift and your passenger could turn out to be a terrific co-traveler and companion, or, instead, could take you on a detour to painful places and a trail of hurts you hadn't anticipated.

But one thing is certain—you can keep driving, gaining ground, despite unfortunate, even destructive, setbacks and events in your life. How do I know this? Because, despite eight years of sexual molestation and abuse at the hands of my father that began when I was nine years old, today I am a mother, wife, daughter, sister, friend, and confidante; a spiritual mentor, by helping my students and clients develop their innate ability for self-awareness by releasing their past hurts and unhealthy self-images; and a teacher of personal transformation, meditation, and healing.

I myself have recovered from pain, anger, shame, and grief. I continue on, very aware that twists and turns on this journey will teach me invaluable lessons each day.

Many years after the abuse I suffered and after a few fruitless detours of my own, I married a man I loved and we started a family together. I was cruising along fairly well, and from an external perspective it seemed that I had gotten to a good place and could just get on with a "normal" life. I thought I could blend in with the rest of the world, and I tried. But there were aching, unresolved feelings begging to be recognized. My closely held secrets were screaming for expression, and I longed to show up in the world more authentically, purged of shame and blame. I knew I still had work to do on myself to live my life in the most honest way. My desire to heal was met with a wish to also celebrate the many blessings of this lifetime. Feedback from clients as well as affirming messages from the Universe, by way of synchronicity when living in my truth, convinced me that sharing this journey is my life's work—telling my story and working with others to find their own unique path to forgiveness, healing, and transformation.

My penchant for personal growth began early. As a student of yoga, meditation, and mantra-chanting from the age of five, I witnessed the profound simplicity and healing that can be found in silence. Later in my life, my curiosity in the healing arts led me to discover a variety of meditation techniques that provided firsthand experience and awareness of the potential for deep change within me. These discoveries fostered new spiritual perspectives and practices. I saw for myself that there was hope for me, that healing was in fact possible, and that I had the potential to access the part of myself that could nurture it.

When I began teaching meditation and tools for personal transformation to others, I began to detect a very human quality in my clients: the desire to transcend their deepest wounds. We all do this to survive. They were showing me a mirror. This was the same desire that made me seek teachers and mentors in my life. Some people live out their whole lives without addressing their wounds; maybe they are so accustomed to their pain, they forget the unhealed past is an obstacle to their happiness and peace. Sometimes newer patterns form around that deeply held past and we lose track of what the real cause of our unfulfilled life is. What I have learned from my own experience is that living an unexamined life comes at a price.

At first, many people thought my work with others was only for women, but I have never meant for this to be the case. I have always held an open door to anyone interested in healing and spiritual growth; after all, we are all in this together. Moreover, I always felt that if I exclude men from my work, then who will be there for my father's healing, my brothers' healing, or my husband's, the man who loves me and cares so much for me? Who will be there for the men who have hurt someone through abuse, still carrying their guilt and shame? How about those men who were themselves abused as children and silenced by their parents, as my father was?

I learned my father's story years into my own healing. When my grandparents found out what was happening to him—at his school during the early 1950s—they pulled him out immediately and placed him in another school. Considering the times and the place, it is understandable that that was their way of handling the problem, but how did their choice affect my father's ability to heal and be whole? It is clear it must have affected him negatively, because he spent years making poor choices in his actions and in his relationship with me, his only daughter. Ironically, however, it was also my father who introduced me to my spiritual mentor, who in turn guided much of my own journey in healing and transformation. Thus my father and I recovered on parallel tracks. Today, he is very much a part of my life and has healthy relationships with my husband and my daughters, and I love him as a daughter would her father. I am told that, under the circumstances, this is rare.

I remember my first transformation client was a woman by the name of Susan. She was in her 60s, and I was in my early 30s. At first I would think to myself, *Who am I to be giving spiritual advice to a woman who has seen so much more of life, someone even older than my own mother? Who am I to think I can help her?* Susan was a successful executive at a financial firm, three times divorced and now living with a partner. She was a businesswoman by day and a talented artist and painter by night. She had survived a few setbacks herself, but her inner pain, sadness, and turmoil had never fully healed. She had moved from one relationship to the next, just carrying on in the hope that the next time around her experience would be better.

When Susan sat crying during our session and opened her heart to me, I discovered my ability to stay grounded, centered, and present. My own heart opened and allowed me to see into, and beyond, Susan's pain to provide her with spiritual insights and understanding of the energetic patterns in her life. We talked about how she might consider making some new choices to break through old behaviors and attitudes to create a foundation for a renewed sense of self-love and hope for her future.

And then, one by one, clients, both men and women, came to me with their unique challenges. They shared stories of deep anger, pain, and hidden shame they had not shared previously with anyone. Their trust in me and the safety they felt with me were awe-inspiring. *What an honor*, I thought.

Was this the Universe sending me messages that I was on to something and that this was the beginning, that my life's work had begun? This message became more pronounced as the weekend retreats I offered began. Over the two-day courses, participants had the opportunity to develop inner awareness, experience some relief from their anguish, and share with others at a deeper level than previously. I learned that retreat students' lives were improving dramatically in the weeks and months that followed these weekends; they sent me requests for some type of program or support system that would provide guidance for continuing to build on the new foundation that had been established during the retreat. To honor this request, I developed and launched the yearlong Inner Awareness Manifestation meditation and transformation course, also called the I AM Consciousness Program.

My meditations continued to reinforce my belief that my real work had begun as I continued traveling down the highway of my own journey—wandering, meandering, sometimes stalling. Some of my most profound insights and spiritual messages arrived after I became a mother. From the first moment I looked at the angelic faces of my three little daughters, I realized more than ever that my work needed to be done. They reminded me what wholeness looked like and that it is our birthright as human beings. In the presence of their divine grace, I found myself captivated by pure surrender to love the moment my little baby girls' eyes met mine; entranced, I knew I could never look the other way. They continue to help me practice being present every single day. They are my most valuable teachers.

I do not hold a Ph.D. in psychology or a certification in therapy or counseling. I do not claim to have spent years and years in research or academically evaluating statistics by interviewing others like me who might have endured similar abuse. Some of my learning comes from the many students, clients, and participants I have directly worked with in my retreats, workshops, and classes. But I am a woman walking the walk who has applied a few lessons learned along the way. I believe that at some level, despite our differences and unique histories, we are still bound by a sacred thread. Our lives are woven together by the fabric of our experiences, like a quilt made with different pieces of cloth. We come from various walks of life, but we can come together to create a profound revolution. Just like a beautiful quilt, we can give each other warmth and comfort from the chill of isolation and loneliness in our individual struggles.

I hesitated again and again to start this book. I wondered what it would mean to have all my own history out there. I asked my parents how they would feel about my sharing not only what I went through but what we went through together. Writing it, without a shadow of a doubt, has been the most terrifying thing I have ever done in my life. Chapter after chapter, I had to move through sometimes paralyzing fears of opening my life to all, for all that had been hidden, to now be revealed. But my commitment to transformation and recovery, and my will and determination to serve as a conduit for universal healing, were stronger and bolder than the insecurities that threatened to disrupt my work. Thus, even though I lurched along many a mile, my resolve to bring this book to completion remained undeterred, and I am grateful for my own as well as for our collective human potential to endure.

As I was writing this book I researched other books that have been written on this subject, and it was heartening and humbling to learn about some extraordinary, pioneering work that had been done. I have included a reading list of many of these works at the back of this book. How I wish someone had told me about them 20 years ago! Nevertheless, when I thought about what I had to say in my book that was different, I realized that none of the others spoke of reconciliation after abuse, addressed transformational meditation as a spiritual tool, or emphasized how integral and essential forgiveness is to healing. I believe that our lives are too short to spend plotting revenge. I will not live forever and neither will my father. But I believe that the lessons in this book can endure the passage of time.

In recounting my journey, this book ultimately became a celebration of our ability to transform our lives and feel the power of liberation when we can find our way to forgiveness—for ourselves and for those who may have abused us. I have no wish to portray anyone as a hero or villain, point fingers, take revenge, or humiliate anyone. Instead, I want to honor the humanity, complexity, resilience, strength, and fragility in all of us and underscore how we possess inner power that can allow us to overcome the obstacles that keep us from reaching our fullest potential.

In my work as a spiritual teacher and transformation leader, I have seen many people silently suffering, pushing their pain and anger away and trying hard to accept the disappointments of their unfulfilled lives. Retreat participants and meditation students in my courses have benefitted from encouragement, direction, and the tangible steps they've learned there to become whole, empowered through lasting transformation to reach their fullest potential. It has been an honor to witness how they continue to change their lives for the better. This book will help you do the same. You are ready when you are ready.

I myself am still traveling along, peeling back the layers of my inner awareness, and this book is part of that. You might find my experiences raise more questions than they answer and, if so, in some ways I would be happy if they do; I have found most of my answers by just being with the questions, and it has served me well. I believe you will find the same to be the case. I don't have a magic bullet to "fix" any of us. Instead, I offer techniques to help you live fully, an invitation to drive into the unknown and be willing to explore the questions and complexities that arise during your own personal journey. Teaching and sharing what I have learned have helped me practice what I preach and speak the uncensored—and heretofore unspeakable—truth. I am honored that you are joining me in this quest.

How to Read This Book

These pages represent an amalgam of my personal memoir and tools for healing. My advice would be to read them from start to finish for context and to put things in perspective. I have made the narrative chronological principally because the sequence of events tracks closely with my stages of inner awareness. With that said, if you feel like you want to jump to the practices or the guidelines in Chapter 5, then by all means do so.

Abuse

I was in the fifth grade, and it was time for final exams at school. My older brother and I came down with the chicken pox. That was the bad news. The good news was that because we had done consistently well in school all year long, we were excused from the final exams and thus automatically promoted to the next grade.

My father had been traveling on a business trip and returned one night when we were in the second phase of the illness, leaving us with dry, scabby skin that itched terribly. He asked us not to scratch the scabs as they would leave scars on our skin, and we did our best to obey. As he tucked me into bed that evening, I felt his hand on my leg. He gently began to rub my leg to soothe the skin, and that felt good. A few moments later, his hands reached between my legs. When he touched my vulva I was confused, but it felt good. I remember the sorts of questions and the immediate rationalizing that flooded in. This was a new feeling I was experiencing. I had never been touched this way before and it was Papa— so there could be nothing wrong with this, right? He loved me, and I always felt safe with him. He knew what he was doing, didn't he?

When I was younger, four or five, I would wake up in the mornings and run out to the verandah where he and Mummy would be drinking their morning tea and reading the newspaper. I would cuddle up on his lap, then take a cookie from the tray to dip into his tea, savoring the soft and gooey treat. After five or ten minutes of that morning warmth while I laid my head on his chest, I would get up and go play with my older brother, practice how to ride my bike, or otherwise be on my way.

In the evening when Papa arrived home, he would honk the car horn at the gate with our signature sound—*beep, beep, beep-beep-beep*—and, hearing it, my brother and I would run outside barefoot in excitement to open the gate and greet him. He would let me sit by his side on the driver's seat so I could steer the car into the portico of the house where he would park. I remember those moments with my father, feeling like I was in a cocoon of safety and protection. He would never let any harm come to me; how could he? I was his only daughter, his princess. He was Papa, that's what I called him. I had idolized him.

From this place of trust and adoration, my nine-year-old self did not question his actions when the molestation started. There was no way I could have known how it would change my life. Nor do I think my father and, later, my mother could have suspected the extent of mental and emotional damage that those few minutes of sexual abuse—that continued in on-and-off cycles from that day until I was 17—inflicted on a girl who was only a child. The molestation would last a few days, then stop for a while, and then start again. I never knew when it was going to begin or end. Most days it happened when I was being awakened for school early in the mornings while the rest of my family was asleep, including my mother, who usually woke up after Papa.

I've since learned that, for a period of time, my father conducted his life recklessly and with impaired judgment. He smoked for several years and took to drinking quite heavily. He was probably in his mid to late 30s when he had an affair with my aunt. It was at this same time his abuse of me began. I didn't know about that affair and no one knew that I was being abused either. My learning about the affair would be the last straw that finally broke the camel's back when I turned 18. He strayed from fidelity to my mother several times, crossed many a line, and finally made the grievous error with me that no one, especially a parent, should ever cross.

I tried to convince myself that feeling up their growing daughters was normal behavior for most fathers. After all, my Papa would never do anything that was going to harm me. I even rationalized that my mother, aunts, cousin sisters must have experienced the same treatment. This happened to all girls, didn't it?

By the time I was 17, I had spent almost a decade feeling confused, emotionally torn up, and mentally out of whack. I was exhausted and tired of going around and around in circles, hoping for some form of divine intervention that never arrived. I secretly prayed to my gods and goddesses to cleanse me of my filth. Ganesha, with the head of an elephant and the body of a man, is the god of wisdom and perfection, and Hindus pray to him for the removal of blocks and obstacles in their lives. Lakshmi is the goddess of wealth, prosperity, and abundance, and my personal protector. I never desired riches when I prayed to her—I only wanted to embody her purity and serenity. But somehow, reciting prayers to Ganesha and Lakshmi wasn't working. Neither was burning camphor nor lighting incense in the hope that maybe somehow lightning would strike and everything would miraculously go back to how it was before I had chicken pox. My father and I could be normal again, like the past never happened. I could feel uplifted about myself, not feel like I was dirty and filthy. *Could this all just be a bad dream?* I asked myself.

I wonder if I had already seen enough repressed sexuality in my culture to be left with these abhorrent feelings about myself, whether from the movies of the '70s and '80s that portrayed the Indian woman either as an untouched, virtuous, angelic, porcelain beauty or as a glamorous courtesan who was raised in the brothel and danced and amused rich men while deeply suffering in her heart, pining for true love. All along, the men portrayed patriarchs, heroes, and fighters with noble character, showing their strength in body and mind, men who would do anything for the honor of their family, heritage, and country!

Monsoon Wedding was probably the first and only movie I have seen set in the Indian ethos. Made by Mira Nair, an Indian filmmaker based in New York, the movie featured a young girl to whom I related very closely. At the end, she comes out and tells everyone in the wedding party what the "uncle" had done to her as a little girl. I remember coming home from that movie and locking myself in the bathroom for what seemed like forever, wailing and crying, screaming. There was so much pain, anger, and sadness suppressed within me. Only in my case, the perpetrator of my misery wasn't my uncle and I didn't know whom to go to and tell.

Looking back, I can see how sexually stifled Indian teenagers and college students were. While I was growing up, most schools and colleges were "girls only" or "boys only." I went to a girls' school from fifth grade onwards. Girls and boys mixing in an academic setting was deemed a distraction and inappropriate. According to the policy makers, it was impossible for students of the opposite sex to focus on education in the same physical space. It could just not be done. That powerful was the sexual tension between the youth of India, attributed in part to all the praying men did to Lord Shiva for virility and sexual prowess.

What blows my mind is the sexual segregation of youth based on a cultural belief system that has been inculcated in the Indian psyche for eons: the idea that sex is bad, touch is wrong, all from the land that gave us the *Kama Sutra*, the most ancient text on the art of lovemaking. Some of those very boys caged all day in their boys' schools, once out in the real world, were the ones pinching, groping, and even raping women returning from their girls-only colleges. There is a group of Indian girls called the Acid Girls whose faces have been scorched and deformed by acid thrown on them by men with whom they refused to have sex—taking date rape to a whole other level.

Misogyny has prevailed all over the world for centuries, but in India, one of the many ways it manifested was in the Pavlovian responses of our mothers and grandmothers to sexual misconduct because "we don't talk about those types of things." Their silence has helped fuel the nation's subjugation of women.

India ranks second, following China, for the greatest instances of female feticide. In a culture in which, on one hand, goddesses are considered sacred and holy, on the other a girl child is considered a shame, a desecration of everything held sanctified, and far less desirable than a baby boy. My mother wrote and directed a short film produced by the United Nations for its "Let girls be born" campaign. At school some of our essay topics would be on "Dowry Deaths" and "Bride Burning"—topics no seventh or eighth grader in the Western world has ever had to write about. Young brides were tortured, scorched, and sometimes burned to death if their parents did not give decent dowries at the wedding, which might include a scooter or a car, gold and silk, silver dishes, and even washing machines. Sometimes the demands would increase or even double after the wedding, and the newly married women were not even allowed to visit their families. That, compounded with the conditioning that a good Indian girl *never* wants for anything or *ever* goes back to her parents once she is married, only adds to the burdens of young brides and married women in India. Although these sort of practices are much less common nowadays, they have not been completely eradicated either. Around 9,000 dowry deaths are reported per year; we will never know how many remain unreported.

Ironically, being in a girls-only school did not keep me from being violated. The one place everyone assumed I was safe was at home, with my parents. But for me it was the only place that scared me because I didn't know from day to day what would happen next. I was constantly distracted trying to figure out the permutations and combinations of my level of safety, all while maintaining a quiet calm on the outside, never letting on there was anything making me even the slightest bit uncomfortable.

The malaise our culture's suffocated sexuality caused permeated Indian society throughout education, family, community, art, and media. But there were also brilliant writers, poets, and artists who depicted an uplifted human condition regardless of gender or geographic origin of Indian groups. I was fortunate to meet teachers and mentors later in my life who would help me have new perspective.

At the time, however, I believed my sexual abuse to be my fault, the punishment I was due for my weakness and my powerlessness to deny the sensual pleasure it provided for the few minutes it lasted. I began to hate myself for feeling good while being touched.

When I felt helpless and unable to exercise control, I would blame my father, figuratively point fingers, and assume the role of the victim. Most likely spiraling in and out of depression, I was finding this cycle was beginning to wear me down, getting really old, even for a resigned and increasingly cynical me. Handing over my power repeatedly was not serving me well. My view of intimacy and physical touch between man and woman was already askew. This misalignment multiplied by my low self-esteem made me feel dead on the inside. This was the best strategy to keep my "real" emotions at bay so I didn't have an outburst or nervous breakdown. Despite all of these horrible feelings, I so badly wanted to feel alive again.

I had come to expect little of my present or future self. On most days I was quite gloomy, sad, and temperamental. I am certain that some of what I was going through was normal teenage angst, but my particular life experience heightened it. At the time, I remember justifying my rage with the belief that I had every right to be bitter, lashing out because of what my father had done to me. I thought that I had been given a life-long license to insult him as a way to release some of my anger. But eventually my attitude struck me as unproductive, pitiful, and pathetic; this war of retribution I was waging was inside of me, not just outside, and I wanted my pain, bitterness, and sadness to disappear. I wanted to feel light again. I wanted to snap my fingers, poof!, and see sunny skies.

Now and again, a fairy tale vision of life would flash in front of my eyes, but almost immediately I'd tell myself I was foolish to think I could get there from where I was. Yet I realize now that those flashes represented a dawning inner awareness that the power to take control of my life was within me. It was within me to create my own circumstances and master my own destiny.

My inner struggles borne out of my history only compounded the turmoil of transitioning out of high school. I had no sense of self-worth and, consequently, horrible self-esteem. When kids graduating from my high school were filling out their college applications for engineering and medical colleges, I believed that the only profession I was fit for was prostitution. Good sense prevailed and I ditched the prostitution idea, although the thought did occur. My fertile mind then came up with a different idea to escape India, my father mainly—maybe I could move to the United States on a student visa. I became a member of the United States embassy library so I could spend hours every day during the summer of the year I graduated high school trying to figure out which colleges in the U.S. I could apply to and how to go about it. There were tests like the Standard Aptitude Test (SAT) and Test of English as a Foreign Language (TOEFL) that I was supposed to take. We did not have career counselors in high school in India, and my parents never had a conversation with me about what I wanted to do with my life. It seemed to me that others had their careers picked out for them. I felt quite alone and overwhelmed by all the research and information I was gathering. I am certain there were others like me, confused and lost; I just did not know who they were.

For some reason, oceanography stood out as a subject of interest to me—that, and drama therapy. They were completely unrelated fields, but both became passions of mine. I loved chemistry, mainly because the high school teacher I had had for the subject inspired me. She also commanded respect while being equally respectful to her students, a quality not all my teachers possessed. I was drawn to drama therapy because it combined psychology with theater, and both subjects were very interesting to me. My parents had met doing theater, and they continued to be involved. Hence I was always naturally drawn to the stage since the day I was born. Theater had always been a part of my life. I also figured my own life experiences and time spent pretending might be an asset. I ended up with fliers and folders from the embassy on the entire how to's. I tried to fumble through the application process by myself, but it was a daunting task, one that I was not equipped to handle without help. Slowly but surely I started to run out of time to apply abroad. In addition, I remember my father clearly saying I wasn't going.

And so I applied to random colleges locally without a plan just because that was what was expected of anyone graduating from high school. I did my best to get in somewhere and earn a bachelor's degree, because *any* bachelor's degree was better than no degree. It was a sign to the community that you were succeeding and accomplishing the goals expected of you, and it was equally a reflection of your parents' success. I went through the motions, applied to colleges, and tried my best to seem normal despite my troubled past, while my parents adopted the "Let's try and ignore these problems and maybe they will go away" strategy.

The fact that my father abused me in such a way was unacceptable, of course, but for appearances' sake, my father, and my mother once she learned the truth, simply pretended it never happened. They did not know how to get help or give help. They were so torn apart, tattered, and confused themselves that the only plan they had was to look the other way and wait until the situation sorted itself out. But the situation, of course, just happened to be my *life*.

My leaving home at eighteen set the stage for transformation at home. My mother helped me relocate and my father helped pay for it. My friends and family saw me as the rebellious teenager who wanted to go against the grain and live life on her terms. No one, of course, knew that the real reason I was leaving home was to escape abuse.

I justified my father's financial contribution to pay for my flight out of town and cover my costs elsewhere as a way to make him pay, literally *pay*, for his transgressions. *Yep, he'd better, after being far from stellar as a father, he'd better pay for it!* I was so angry, vehemently angry in my teenage years. Curses directed at him sat on the tip of my tongue, ready to fly at any moment. He was a far cry from the man that I, as an innocent child who had trusted her father, had lovingly called Papa.

The chicken pox had indeed left a scar. It sits right in the middle of my forehead, the site of the third eye chakra that is the center of intuition and wisdom. In the Indian belief system, the chakra system is set of seven chakras aligned to the central line of the human body through which all of one's energy flows. I don't think this scar on my third eye chakra was a coincidence. This was the beginning of the shame, guilt, anger, pain, and loneliness that would haunt me for nearly 20 years and significantly affect my ability to trust myself or trust others. I developed an intensified fear of the unknown and a damaging view of myself as worthless and undeserving.

RETREAT CASE

In my retreats, I have met and worked with several men and women who were abused, even assaulted, during their childhoods. Several were well into their 50s and 60s and had not broken their silence until the retreat. Abuse has inflicted a combination of punitive, mental, or sexual harm on innocent people at the hands of men or women whom the victim trusted—a relative, parent, stepparent, older sibling, cousin, or neighbor. Some of these exploited people had been in therapy for decades, yet they remained stuck, unable to reconcile, accept, and forgive their abusers or their own shame and guilt.

In the safe space I create for them, retreat participants are gently invited to pause and be silent observers of their own lives to perceive what is true for them. I have watched them get in touch with their old, suppressed, unhealed memories and emotions while they confronted their truth as if for the first time. I have seen their sometimes-cathartic release of anger, pain, and shame they'd pent up for decades. Once freed of old baggage that had been weighing them down, the participants were able to access their compassion and open their hearts. They transformed, no longer controlled by their anger as they entered a softer, more receptive space where they could be gentle and kind with themselves. Every retreat has left me feeling most grateful for being a facilitator for these participants and honored to be in the presence of such deep healing and transformation. My belief that we all can heal from our deepest wounding is continually restored and reinforced as participants discover their innate power to love and forgive unconditionally.

Commentary

The experiences we have as children mold, at the deepest level, the way we view ourselves as adults. As the movies of our past replay continually, frame by frame, we become conditioned to believe that this is how life is. This belief becomes our way of being. Past experiences, what was said to us and how we were left feeling, become integral influences on our inner voice. We respond to life based on what this voice tells us, which speaks to us in ways consistent with our wounding. Those people who have been raised with an abundance of positive conditioning and reinforcement make very different choices from others of us who, like me, became convinced we were never good enough, no matter how hard we tried. There are observable differences in the language we use and the relationships we attract into our lives.

Our inner dialog is the light that illuminates the path we choose in life, a path whose coordinates mark our journey's twists and turns. Whether we live a life that is based in fear or in love, how we support or advise others, the words we choose—all are informed by our inner dialog. If you believe the old adage that all good things must come to an end, as I did, then you will always be looking for the next dark cloud to appear. If you believe that you will never be a success, then you will likely set expectations of yourself so high that you are sure to fail or even be unable to recognize your achievements along the way. Either way, the self-sabotage will continue until you pause, face your truth, and actively choose a different way.

Questions for Self-Introspection

•	Are there experiences or events from your childhood or your past that have become movies that replay over and over again in your mind?
•	Do you still have a visceral emotional response when you remember events from your life that left you feeling bad, mad, or sad about yourself and your life?
•	Are there certain people or someone specific associated with this past with whom you feel incomplete and long to have closure?
•	If you take a few minutes to sit in silence and witness your inner dialog, your inner voice, how does that leave you feeling? Does it raise you up or bring you down?
•	When you think about your life, are you left feeling hopeful or hopeless, empowered or disempowered, happy or sad?
•	Do you believe your past and the people associated with it are forgivable or are they undeserving of forgiveness?

Denial

*The worst lies are the lies we tell ourselves. We live in denial
of what we do, even what we think. We do this because
we're afraid.*

—Richard Bach

My mother felt like it was time to have a big-girl talk with me
shortly after my 13th birthday, so one afternoon after school
she sat me down face-to-face in our dining room. I will never
forget the scene: the lighting in the room, the position of the chairs, where
I was sitting, what I was wearing. The image is still etched in my memory.

She asked me, "Has any boy ever tried to kiss you?" And I replied,
very matter of factly, that the only boy who had ever kissed me was Papa.
She laughed.

"That's not the kind of kiss I meant, silly. I mean like any boy you
know, or a boyfriend."

I thought for a moment, but no one other than Papa came to mind.
When I looked up at her awaiting my answer, I knew something was
wrong, like something big was about to explode. The tone of my voice
dropped as fear flooded my throat. As sincerely as I could, I looked
Mummy straight in her eyes and said, "Ma, the only boy who ever kissed
me is Papa."

There was a dead silence.

I began to tell her about the summer I had chicken pox and what had
been happening since then. I even told her how I assumed it was normal
and that she must have been shown love in a similar fashion.

I waited for her to respond. I had no idea what to expect, and still, even today, her reaction surprises me. She was disbelieving, thought that I was making it up, and suggested that I had just said this to get attention. She said that ever since my younger brother was born, I'd complained I felt ignored by my parents, claiming they paid a lot of attention to him and spoiled him. She even suggested that I might have an Electra complex—Carl Jung's theory of psychosexual development positing that a daughter competes with her mother for the love, or possession, of her father.

Wow! I had no freaking idea what she meant, but it was clear that she discounted my words entirely and I would just have to wait to see what happened after my parents discussed my revelation. I remember feeling sidelined—like I was secondary to my father's primary position of trust in all circumstances, even this. It was confusing. I had never experienced sadness so profound until that day. Our discussion ended with my mother saying that she would talk to Papa that evening.

The moments after our discussion were torture. Absolute torture. *What if he says I am lying? What will I do? Will they throw me out of the house? Where will I go?*

To my mother's credit, she did talk to my father, in private. To his credit, he didn't deny it. She came to me and simply said, "He says he is sorry and that he will never do it again." She also made me promise that I would never, *ever*, reveal this to a single person.

"You can't tell *anyone*, OK, Richa? *Especially* your brothers—at least let *them* have a clean and pure relationship with their father."

Phew! Was I relieved? Hardly! So all that had happened for the previous years was over, huh? Just like that. Wow! That was smooth and easy. All cleaned and tied up with a nice pretty bow. Neat!

I didn't know what else to do but agree and honor her request. This was my mother, and I was supposed to do whatever she asked me to do, no questions asked. She was adamant that I never hurt my brothers by my behavior or let what she called my "impurity" dirty them. And so we never discussed it again.

Because it was clear my mother would not support me if I broke my promise, I had no will to stand up for myself. The next time my father made an advance, I didn't resist. The touch felt good, and the attention I was getting felt good too. All this had to stay a secret anyway, so why not go ahead and accept it? I was getting used to being aroused in this way. *How does any of this matter anymore?* These sexual interactions with my father coupled with the strict order from my mother were a treacherous blend that I am certain played a role in causing confusion and conflict in my psychosexual development. No type of abuse is OK, but in sexual abuse something that is supposed to feel good is turned into something horrible—this is one of its terrible paradoxes. I was beginning to believe that I really *was* dirty, impure, and worthless, just like my mother implied, and I created my own evidence of this with the choices I made.

And so, for the next four years, the abuse continued and my parents crafted a remarkably well-maintained facade of normalcy between them and me as well as between each other. Meanwhile, my shame grew deeper and the darkness within me blacker. Up until this unprecedented situation with my father, his touch had always been something good; now, although it often *felt* good, the touch that had to remain a well-kept secret was also a source of profound shame for me.

I spent hours pondering my mother's insistence on secrecy, and what I had seen in her eyes and heard in her voice was fear. Deep fear, terror. I felt trapped like a caged bird, wingless, mute, and without a song. *How would others view my parents if word got out that this was going on? What would happen to her and her three children without the financial support our lifestyle demanded and the conveniences it offered?* In our culture, it would be seen as an immensely shameful thing for someone like her, a married woman in India, to leave her husband and return to her parents' home. The shame would be even greater for her parents. As long as her husband was going to support the family, she would have to ignore my revelation.

Besides, I'm sure she believed him when he apologized and said he wouldn't do it again. She seemed sure of it, probably fearing for the survival of her way of life, which was now under threat; her panic wouldn't let her believe anything else. Food, shelter, clothing, education, and every other material thing needed to raise a family were justifications for letting this transgression pass, limitless excuses to bury our secret forever.

It has always been very important to my mother that our family members be in harmony, that we were "one big, happy family." She tried and tried, arduously. She planned vacations, picnics, and family portraits. Everyone who saw us in the community complimented her on what a lovely family she had, and she glowed with that acknowledgment. She'd feel like she had succeeded simply if a stranger, like a waiter in a restaurant, had been approving.

This may be part of the reason my mother's tendency to deny everything wrong in her marriage began early in my parents' relationship. Married at 19, she had loved only my father and dedicated herself to him. He, however, had at times behaved in ways that caused her concern; his interest in other women at social gatherings seemed excessive at times, and his refusal to explain some odd absences from home caused her to worry about his faithfulness.

She also struggled with depression and mood swings. I recall coming home from school one day and finding her asleep in her bed; she had deliberately overdosed on sleeping tablets in an unsuccessful suicide attempt. She did not seek treatment and she did not talk about it. Many years later I discovered what led her to that point, but at the time, being only 10 years old, I didn't know what to think. All I knew was that my parents had been fighting a lot after my abuse had begun and I did not make the connection. I noticed that she was very unhappy. This was in the early '80s, and the problems a prosperous married woman in Indian society might have had with her husband were never discussed. The *honor* of the family was at stake. So, like always, we pushed this incident away and never spoke of it, ever. My mother never went in for any type of therapy or counseling in the aftermath either. That was not what women did—the shame and stigma attached to emotional pain, suffering, and mental health were very much an issue then as they are now, with only subtle improvements in recent years. Her depression, denial, and suppressed rage emerged partly in the form of overeating and weight gain. My parents also often fought behind closed doors, and my brothers and I could hear the sounds of the slapping and beatings my father inflicted on her for speaking out and fighting for herself. All of this traumatized us kids and, in my case, compounded my stress.

Yet my mother, somehow, strangely, would always bounce back with a cheerful and happy disposition. She could be depressed, quiet, and sulking for days, giving only monosyllabic answers with wide, listless eyes. And then suddenly, like the fog had lifted off of her, she would shine bright like the sun. I remember her as a jokester, entertainer, excellent cook, and great listener. I loved cuddling with her in the early mornings. I would wake up in my bedroom, go crawl into bed with her to wrap my

leg and arm over her, and get those extra minutes of sleep in the morning. They were the best 10 minutes of my day. She was so cuddly and
warm. At those times, I felt like the luckiest girl on the planet with the
best mother in the world.

She and I used to go out on "dates." We loved to go to the Mercara, a
local coffee shop in The Chola, a five-star hotel near our home. We would
get chicken sandwiches and cold coffee, which in India is a delicious coffee milkshake with a scoop of vanilla ice cream in it. The drinks came in
tall glasses with a long spoon, and I loved to eat the vanilla ice cream
first and then drink the cold coffee with the straw.

We would take our time and chat. It was at these times that she would
ask me about my life, crushes, friends, and school. She would very
smoothly and easily get it all out of me. She was my best friend. I didn't
feel like I needed friends in school because I had her. I loved my mother
more than anything or anyone in the world.

My relationship with her was the *only* one in my life in which I wasn't
hiding behind a veil. I felt like she loved me despite my dirt. I needed her.
I wanted her to love me. What we had felt sweet and special, and unconsciously, I think, I wanted that piece of my life to stay intact. I believe
that's why I felt like I needed to listen to her and do as she had asked me
the day I told her about the abuse. I wanted to please my mother; she
loved me and of course I was her baby. She believed that what she was
doing was the best solution for me at the time. When she made me promise her I would never tell anyone, not even my brothers, I agreed. I never
told a soul until much later—when silence was no longer an option.

When I was very young, before the abuse my father inflicted on me
had begun, I suffered two episodes of sexual molestation. I never told
anyone about them, and I've often wondered if those experiences may
have persuaded me that my father's exploitation might have been some-
what normal and not all that unusual. In any event, I had some practice
now hiding my own sexual victimization, so my mother's request for
secrecy did not seem too surprising.

I was five years old during one of our family vacations to the mountains, and our cousin's sister, who was around 16, was traveling with us.
My father was working through the week and would be joining us later,
so our chauffeur drove us. One day he took me behind some shrubs to
fondle and molest me orally. Next he asked me to peer at my cousin
through the bathroom door's keyhole while she was taking a shower,

then come to him with the details. I don't recall telling him anything, but I did peek at my cousin as she bathed; I had no idea why other than the fact that I had been asked to—and I already had learned that you don't say no to your elders, not even the family driver. I stayed away from him after that. I never told anyone, not so much because I thought what happened was wrong or that I had something to hide, but more because I didn't think it was important enough—it had already cost me a precious amount of playtime.

During my childhood, my mother worked freelance intermittently as a voice artist, theater director, playwright, and copywriter for ad agencies. It wasn't so much about earning money as it was about keeping her abundant creativity alive and putting it to good use. She was respected in her field and often traveled to attend engagements. When she would leave for her jobs, my brothers and I would be in the care of servants, chauffeurs, and maids.

On one such occasion, when I was around seven, my brothers and I were in the care of our maid who also served as our nanny/governess when our parents were both at work. One day our neighbor's chauffeur's son was allowed to visit. He was probably 11 or 12. We were playing hide and seek, and it was my brother's turn to count. I found a narrow spot between a headboard and the wall to squeeze into, then lay down on the floor. The chauffeur's son saw me, so he crawled onto me, pulled out his penis, yanked down my panties, and rubbed himself on me. To get away, I tried pushing him off, but I had literally gotten myself into a tight spot. I felt terrified and helpless.

As an adult, 20 years of transformation and healing later, I have peeled back the layers between what I now understand to be the truth and the perspective of the child I had once been. Over time, I have been able to have compassion for my mother as a woman, wife, daughter, sister, *and* mother. She always used to say to me, "You will understand when you become a mother, Richa. You will understand why I had to stay with your father. Why such decisions are not that easy. Why I am right in the choices I am making. Why this has to remain a secret forever."

And one day I *did* become a mother, but then, for the life of me, I could not understand *how* my mother had lived with herself all the years of not protecting me as a mother should have. All along I had considered my mother to be my best friend and my confidante. Now, as a mother myself, I questioned with every fiber of my being the integrity of her motherhood. *How could she have allowed this? How could she not do anything to help me after hearing the truth? Why didn't she send me to my grandmother? Or send me to boarding school? Was she such a weak woman that she couldn't make that decision for me? Were family name, money, and reputation more important than me? Why didn't she help me? Why, why, why?*

I had always wanted to be like my mother—I loved her vivacity, joie de vivre, creativity, and abounding inner light and spirit. But after my abuse and her underwhelming response as my protector, I started to see the image of my role model crumble a little bit at a time. The woman whom I once adored and worshipped was weak, and I never wanted to be that. In time I realized there was little I had in common with the woman who had brought me into the world. She was cowardly, disempowered, and lacking a modicum of self-respect. It was clear; I decided I *never* wanted to be like her. I hadn't realized it then, but in reality, my relationship with my mother was my biggest blind spot.

My father, while still continuing to molest me, turned toward religion. He never explained why; perhaps it was to cleanse himself or to feel virtuous, or maybe to gain respect from others because he was ashamed of himself. In any case, he became extremely fanatical in his theological demands. He dictated that the entire family go to a school that was based in religious teaching, and he insisted we attend the religious community meetings he was a part of on Sunday mornings. To please him and not create any ripples, we all, albeit begrudgingly, obeyed, and year after year kept up false appearances. It was around this time that Michael Jackson's song "Man in the Mirror" was released. I remember the first time I heard it on my cassette player. I rewound it over and over again and wrote each and every lyric down, and I related most intensely to the one that goes, "If you want to make the world a better place, take a look at yourself and make that change." When I sang along, I had the odd sensation that a block of sadness that had been lodged in my throat for a long time was slowly melting. I'd cry singing along to this song, directing these lyrics in my mind toward my father.

A few years before he became so religious, my father had been a heavy drinker and smoker. My brothers and I found it very difficult to digest the fact that suddenly one day he was giving us sermons on how to live our lives ethically and virtuously. He wore white from head to toe six days a week. My mother starched and laundered these clothes and laid them out for him every morning in their room. Meanwhile, he continued to abuse me. This man who was sexually molesting his only daughter was also the person who, when I was 22 years old, would introduce me to the person who became my spiritual mentor and guide for the next 16 years, when I was at the lowest point in my life. My life would not have been the same without my spiritual mentor in it and I would not have met her if it weren't for my father. Life has an interesting way of connecting the dots.

My father ultimately became a priest and began serving the community with very well-written and well-spoken sermons. He has been one of the most popular priests in the community because of his ability to explain the Vedic principles with wit and humor—his theater background coming in handy. He was also a mechanical engineer, a graduate of one of the most highly reputed universities in India, IIT (Indian Institute of Technology). He was a highly educated, intellectual, generous, and caring person. I wondered what happened to him that caused a man with these attributes to commit such dreadfully exploitative acts.

For many years I lived behind a superficial veil of lies, supposedly sheltered from the harm that would come from sharing my truth. The truth, I was made to believe, would shake up the very foundation of our lives, the perception that we were the happiest family ever seen. There was a safety in this subterfuge and fierce danger in the truth. Denying the abuse was key to survival, an awareness that quickly became ingrained from the moment it had begun.

This secret lurking in my life affected my judgments and choices, and caused me to internalize a distorted view of myself. It lay so deeply within me that there were times I would tell myself nothing had really happened. I was over-reacting, being melodramatic and ego-

At the approach of danger there are always two voices that speak with equal forces in the heart of man: one very reasonably tells the man to consider the nature of the danger and the means of avoiding it; the other even more reasonable says that it is too painful and harassing to think of the danger, since it's not in a man's power to provide for everything and escape from the general march of events; and that it is therefore better to turn aside from the painful subject till it has come, and to think of what is pleasant. In solitude a man generally yields to the first voice; in society to the second.

—Leo Tolstoy, *War and Peace*

tistical, even making the whole story up. Acknowledging the abuse even to myself would mean reliving the shame, anger, pain, and guilt repeatedly and damaging the family system I was sworn to protect. It would mean living with the rawness of how I felt every moment. I did not know what to do with that, where to go with it, and how to process the feelings associated with my true emotional state. It was easier, *much* easier, to pretend and to deny.

I was wedded to this uncomfortable comfort zone. Divorcing it was not an option. I had taken a vow, promised my mother. Now, my silence and I were together forever, until death do us part. I was to live and stay in denial, accepting the fearfully modified version of the truth as my truth, not just for my best interest but for the highest good of all—my parents, brothers, extended family, and the family name.

Heaven forbid my truth inconvenience a distant relative on the other side of the planet. What would they think? How would this news impact my aging grandparents? Haven't they been through enough? They have fought for Indian freedom, gone to jail, rallied with Mahatma Gandhi; do they need to know all this?

I convinced myself I needed to take one for the team! As I look back on that time in my life, I can finally grasp how much energy I spent trying not to get found out for being who I really was. I was beyond sad; I was bereft and in a very dark place.

Not knowing what to do with the torrent of confusion in my heart and mind, I listened to music and, locked in my bedroom, danced myself to distraction until I was in a pool of sweat, exhausted. I listened to the same song a hundred times, much as I had done with the Michael Jackson tune, and wrote the lyrics down until they inked themselves on my brain. Other days, when the emotions were too overwhelming, I would lock myself in again, this time in the bathroom, and just bawl, curled up in a fetal position. Looking at myself in the mirror would make me want to throw something at the image. My self-hatred was pronounced, and my visceral reaction of disgust and loathing when I saw my reflection was frightening.

There were days I didn't even want to live anymore. I just wanted to end the pain, end the persistent nausea, end the pretense that my life and I were OK. On the days that I crumbled to the bathroom floor, crying for hours, I felt an inconsolable ache but no words to articulate my feelings. During my crying fits, my mother would keep knocking on the door.

"Richa, Richa, Rich . . . Rich . . . open the door. Please, Rich, open the door."

And I couldn't. I would just scream and cry louder to drown her out.

"Leave me alone, just leave me alone," I would yell. *You have left me alone anyway. Why do you pretend to care now?*

After a time, my gloom would pass temporarily and I would return to my socially acceptable, seemingly well-adjusted self, just another teenager going through typical teenage stuff.

I focused my energy in school on sports, music, dance, theater, and debate teams. I was all over the place trying to overreach and overachieve to compensate for the not-so-good feelings within. Seeking recognition on the outside, even being celebrated by strangers, emerged from my ever-increasing need for external validation to balance the powerful self-disapproval gnawing away inside. I won most of the competitions I entered in chess, dance, swimming, singing, and theater. I became the cultural secretary of my high school.

In addition, if this wasn't enough, I had a professional career outside of school. I had been doing voiceover work, or dubbing, for commercials and films from the age of five. I'd also worked as a child actress and voice artist. I was good at these pursuits and remember really enjoying them. My first television commercial was for an electronics company called Keltron that made television sets. I recall the thrill of watching myself on screen for the first time when my family and I were in a movie theater to watch Walt Disney's *The Jungle Book* and I appeared in a commercial (in India, commercials ran in theaters as well as on TV). Suddenly people around me began to recognize me, saying, "That was you, you were just in that ad!" As a very young girl, I found this terribly exciting.

My mother was also involved as a director in a theater group she started herself. There were rehearsals every evening at home, and three to four professional theater productions were staged out of our home every year. These would also keep me busy. So if I wasn't studying or competing at school, I'd appear either on stage or behind the scenes as a stagehand for the rehearsals my mother held at my local high school. Other times, I just made tea for the cast and crew at home. (My tea was pronounced the best rehearsal chai; I'd put cardamom, cloves, and ginger into boiling water, add black tea leaves and milk, boil for a good five minutes, then add sugar and boil the mixture some more to dissolve the sugar. Then I'd strain the tea, pour it into thermos flasks, and ride over to the high school. I would also make a second flask of sugarless tea for me; I never drank my tea sweetened.)

Throughout high school, I coupled my interest in theater with a desire to study psychology, dreaming I would be a therapist or counselor with a Ph.D. one day. My curiosity and inquisitiveness about human behavior sparked questions: *Why do people act the way they act? How does a therapist help people feel better about themselves? What makes people do certain things, take certain actions in the course of their life?* I thought that it would be the best, most productive way of achieving two objectives with one effort: earning a socially acceptable, even celebrated, distinction with my education, and maintaining a very good facade—to hide my internal, damaged self—for my grandparents, extended family, and everyone else. In the back of the lab, the hidden "I" who lived my "real life" could be fixing myself, maybe discovering the magic bullet that would get me out of my misery. I was hopeful, being proactive in seeking a solution. Shifting my thoughts in this manner was refreshing. *I am onto something. I can get myself out of the mess I am in.*

When I graduated high school, I was accepted to Women's Christian College in Chennai, India, a prestigious undergraduate college offering a degree in psychology. I was so excited and happy. I couldn't stop dancing for joy for days. Freedom from living a life of shame was around the corner. Life was finally beginning to turn. Help was on its way. Soon everything would be set right.

The college's psychology department offered free counseling to its students, so I made an appointment with a faculty professor who served as a counselor. After an hour-long session in which she listened to what I had to say, she offered no real advice, helped me chart no course. So I made another appointment with a different professor, but she just sat there and at the end of the session, got up and left without a word. I made a third appointment. When our time was up, this professor actually had something to say:

"This is your family matter. You should ask your parents to help you."

Apparently she did not see the irony in that, so it didn't take me long to realize that I was at a dead end. These teachers, who were supposedly there to help guide and teach future psychologists how to counsel people like me out in the real world, could not even help a student seeking real-life support.

Since my appeals for help failed, I wrote a 24-page letter to my college principal, as they are called in India, explaining the pain I was in and asking for help. She did not respond. I was devastated. I truly wanted to study psychology to serve others as well as to heal myself. But it was not meant to be.

My earlier triumphs in high school were soon becoming a distant memory. I had started out my first year of college with high levels of enthusiasm. But when the support I thought I would find there did not materialize, I began to lose hope, feel lonely and depressed. I felt like I did not fit in. I was beginning to lose my passion for tennis, basketball, dance, and theater. I was listless, low on energy, and gaining weight. My once high-energy, uplifted spirit of my school years was slowly sinking. I felt like a small fish in a big pond—something that many first-year students in college probably feel—but in addition, I felt abandoned and betrayed on all fronts. I was in one of the best colleges in South India, in its most sought-after department, about to study a subject that I had been dreaming of pursuing since ninth grade, and I was still lost.

I was writing poetry: "Past black, present grey, future black / I don't know where I am going, but my bags are packed . . ." I didn't see any point in carrying on. I began having suicidal thoughts; I wanted to end my life.

I started dropping out of classes. I would wake up in the morning and leave home and get on the bus, but would get off halfway and go to a friend's house. Even though he wasn't home, I'd let myself in, take a nap, listen to music, waste my time until the afternoon, and go home. Pretend, keep secrets, and lie. It got easier by the day.

My friends never questioned my weirdness. They just loved me for who they thought I was and never suspected anything. I had done a great job of appearing normal and had everyone fooled—except me.

Because my attendance the first year of college was so abysmal, the very faculty members who had failed to help me when I needed it refused to let me take my finals; they said I had to make up all my classes before I could earn the privilege of writing the exams. Given how intensely unhappy I was and my suicidal depression, the inconvenience of attending classes had seemed overwhelming. It was just not worth my time and attention, but the psychology department obviously didn't see it that way. I was trying desperately to figure out how I was going to make it through my life, but I didn't have any motivation and didn't know where to turn anymore. The anger, resentment, and shame kept building inside me like a pressure cooker ready to explode. I was carrying a burden that was eating me; I felt restless, agitated, and lacked any sort of focus. I dropped out of college and later completed my bachelor's via a correspondence course after I moved to New Delhi—around a year after I left home.

My dysfunctional behavior earned me a reputation for being a wild one, a bohemian vagabond, an arrogant and aggressive "bad apple." These opinions, despite their negativity, coalesced into a great protective device. Seeming reckless and out of control was the Krazy Glue that helped me hold it all together so that the forbidden truth never escaped my lips.

Nevertheless, my self-destructive ways would inevitably lead to an implosion. I had started smoking cigarettes that my father and the actors frequenting the house for rehearsals had left lying around. In fact, my father himself would give me cigarettes to smoke and watch me while I did. I must have been six or seven years old. Also, in secret, I'd started to drink alcohol and experiment with recreational drugs. And once the music was turned on, I was up on my feet and danced like a maniac to release all the pent-up emotion. Dance was my best release. It let me free myself from all the mental, emotional, and physical tension. But it was just a temporary fix, like a Band-Aid. How could I create a more lasting feeling of peace within myself? I decided I needed a more permanent plan to take the pressure off of living a duplicitous life.

That's when I came up with my first plan—Plan A. I felt like it was time to finally act on my suicidal thoughts and put an end to the pain. I considered consuming an excessive amount of sleeping pills like my mother had or slitting my wrists or jumping off of a tall building like I had seen in a movie. Plan A failed, obviously, as I never managed to do myself in, though I did slit my wrist one time—not deep enough.

Still hoping there was a way out of feeling miserable, I thought of a second plan—Plan B. One night I walked into my parents' bedroom and watched them while they lay sleeping. I wondered what would happen if I just killed my father? *Wouldn't that make my life easier?* I wondered how I would do it. *Should I use the pillow? Should I buy rat poison?* I remember jogging my brain for ideas. But in seeing my mother asleep beside my father, instead of the bubbly, humorous, and fun-loving woman that I knew her to be once, I saw a weak, pathetic, and helpless woman. *How would she cope if he were dead? Does he have a life insurance policy?*

Will it be enough for her to get by and put my brothers and me through school and college? Would this work? Could it finally give me peace? As I watched them I remember thinking how warm and loving I had once felt toward them. But in that moment I felt hardened and stone cold.

I remember thinking of my two brothers. *What will happen to them? They don't deserve to be denied the life they are supposed to have. I should not and cannot do anything that could jeopardize their future. They have done nothing wrong.* I talked myself out of it and slowly stepped out of my parents' room and went back to bed.

After a while I came to terms with the fact that Plan A to kill myself or Plan B to kill my father were both actions I would never take. It would have to be Plan C, which required that I wait for Papa to die a natural death. I would just go on pretending until then. When he finally died, then, only then, I would begin to heal myself, speak my truth, and live my life.

The following summer, when I was 18 years old, brought with it news of loss. My uncle, my father's oldest brother, died at age 55 of a heart attack. My uncle and I had been very close and he doted on me. Although he lived in Valencia, Spain, and we didn't meet that often, he called me every weekend and talked to me about my life, school, and friends, and our conversations were effortless. Every Sunday morning, I waited eagerly, and when the phone rang, we all knew it would be him.

Losing him was surreal. In my heart of hearts, I had come to think of him as my father. Neither he nor my own father knew this. All the love and caring that I wanted to share with my own father were reserved for Sunday mornings when I talked to my uncle who had become my refuge. I called him Bhapey, which in Punjabi (a North Indian language) means "older brother." Growing up, my uncle's younger siblings, including my father, called him that, so I did too. He loved it, so much so that when I was old enough to realize I was using the wrong name and attempted to correct myself, he refused to let me.

Immediately after he died, I reacted to my devastation with numbness. I didn't emote, I didn't express, and I didn't openly grieve. I just sat like a statue made out of stone for days. He was alive just the other day and then he was gone.

At my grandmother's home where we assembled for the funeral, my younger brother and I ended up making a quick trip to see my maternal uncle, Ramesh, visiting from California. He had four daughters, and, since I had no sisters, I was pretty close to them. In our childhood we had spent our summers together at our grandma's house. But for the past seven years, we had been forbidden from meeting with them or from talking or writing letters to them. We didn't know why. No one would tell us. Regardless, I now had made this trip to visit with them and see if there was any way we could connect again.

Being with them seemed to put us right back where we left off. I immediately reconnected with my cousins and was for the first time considering opening up about my past. Being away from home and my parents, spending time with my oldest cousin-sister, somehow gave me the comfort and freedom to share my secret. She and I went for a long walk after dinner, and little by little, I told her everything. I remember hesitating at first, but then slowly started to share with her how and when the sexual abuse began, my not knowing what to do, my feelings of confusion. I was very nervous because I did not know how she would react. And at the same time I was breaking my promise to my mother—that was a big step for me as it was something I thought I would never do. I still remember her expression to this day. There was shock, horror, and anger all in one expression. She looked like she was ready to kill my father herself. She grabbed my hand in hers and said, "Let's go back to the house right now! Come with me, we need to tell Papa [her dad, my uncle]."

I didn't know what to expect. *What was going to happen now? What have I done? Is this good or bad?* Part of me was still processing that *I just told someone.* It all happened so quickly; I couldn't believe that the secret that had governed my life for so long was out in the open in a matter of minutes. I remember my heart fluttering in happiness for a few moments and I was feeling something new in myself—something rare. *Is this what speaking your truth feels like?* I was excited and at the same time shocked at myself. Space with my cousin had somehow allowed me to open up, and everything just poured out of me. I had never felt so raw and opened up before.

What deepened the importance of my visit to my cousins was learning why our parents had separated our families for all these years. My cousin-sister revealed to me that my father and her mother had had an affair. If there wasn't enough going on in my life already, it was this knowledge that finally "broke the camel's back" of my withheld emotions.

My tears flowed uncontrollably and kept coming for 11 days straight. I barely spoke. All I did was cry. The feelings, thoughts, and emotions kept pouring out of me with my tears through the floodgates that had opened. I feared I was having a nervous breakdown. My uncle and my cousins could not believe I had kept this hidden for so long. I knew they all felt sorry for me. It was bad enough that my father had an extramarital affair with their mother, but that he had been sexually abusing me was unfathomable.

My Uncle Ramesh was the first person to give me any sensible and circumspect advice. "Your mother can't do anything. She is trapped in what society and community want and expect her to be. You need to leave home and make a life for yourself. If you want, I will buy you a ticket to come to the U.S. with me. But *you* must do something."

Up until this time I had never felt like I had permission to leave home or that it was even an option. I was an unmarried Indian girl and this was the early '90s. Leaving home at 18 was unheard of, even for a boy, let alone a single girl. Even nowadays, girls stay home until it is time to marry—although this is changing. But my uncle was right: only I could do something.

I felt an inner power awaken within me when he told me I needed to do something, make a life for myself. I remember thinking, in that moment, that if I chose to stay and leave things the way they were, I would be miserable. If I chose to leave, with no idea where to go, what to do, or how to plunge into the unknown abyss, there would be hope that something good might happen. That helped me realize there was no alternative; I needed a fresh start.

When I came home, I declared my intentions to my mother—who then, in our customary family style, conveyed this to my father. I wasn't asking if I could leave. I was leaving. I had made my mind up and this wasn't up for discussion. That was it. I had little to nothing to say to them. I packed an overnight bag and moved to my friend Vini's home. I stayed as far away from home as I could to avoid having to look at my father's face. I had told my mother what I had learned on my recent visit to her brother's house—that he knew and that I was not going to stay at home any more. I was convinced that moving almost 1,500 miles away was what I needed to do to resurrect my life. I felt it necessary to get away from constant reminders of the abuse, the chaos and dissonance triggered when I saw the fear in my parents' faces, going to familiar places in town that brought back memories that kept me caged in self-hate. I wanted my life to improve.

My parents had never seen me like this before. They knew I meant it. I wasn't going to change my mind. They reluctantly agreed to help me relocate instead. My mother helped me pack, and my father bought me my airline ticket.

What I didn't expect was how my heart would break to leave my brothers. Growing up, I was especially close to my older brother. He is just a year older than me and we shared every single secret—except, of course, one. When I left, though, it was clear that I could not go without confiding in him. I had already broken my promise to my mother by telling my cousin-sister and uncle. But now I was going to go one step further and tell my brother—something my mother had specifically asked me not to do. I would not leave him in the dark about why his sister had suddenly become so weird. Although my parents never insisted I call him Bhaiya, which means "older brother" in Hindi, I enjoyed using the term then and I still do. I feel a sense of comfort from it because it declares that I am the younger sister whom he cares for, loves, and protects.

When I would have one of my emotional mood swings and would snap at everyone around me, especially my father, Bhaiya would try to calm me down and implore me to reconsider my tone, reminding me that I was being rude and arrogant.

Do you know why I talk to him like that? Do you know what he did? Do you know who he really is?

The fact that Bhaiya hadn't known my secret over the years had really frustrated and saddened me. Several times, I was on the verge of telling him so that he would understand the reason for my behavior. But then I would catch myself and hold my tongue. Like my mother had admonished me, "At least let *them* have a clean and pure relationship with their father."

But not this day, I decided, and I still remember his pain and anger when I told him. He shut his eyes and breathed heavily, bending his head forward in disappointment and sadness. I did not know how to comfort him. I could tell he was devastated. He said he felt like he should have been able to protect me and he didn't. But how could he?

We kept our younger brother out of the loop completely. Although Bhaiya didn't like to do that, we were very protective of him and wanted to save him the confusion. I talked to my younger brother a few years later, and he has since had his own journey of forgiveness with our father.

I felt like the move was all I needed to fix everything. It would remove me from the toxic environment at home and was the first step of the long journey to come in my healing. Without it, I could not have followed any of the other steps. So even though I had to make sacrifices and remove myself from my home, my brothers, my friends, and the lifestyle I was accustomed to, I don't think I would have survived if I hadn't left. It represented the moment I took charge of my life and refused to deny my truth any longer. In hindsight, I see how denial only prolonged the damage to my heart, mind, and spirit. Arising out of a misguided sense of self-preservation, it delayed my facing the truth about myself as well as my parents.

RETREAT CASE

During a retreat, a male participant who had been victimized by a male pedophile once asked, "Why should I forgive him for what he did to me? He is still out there living a so-called respectable life. I can't forgive him until he acknowledges me for having left him alone (that is, not publicly humiliating him)."

"So how long are you willing to wait for this acknowledgment?" I asked him.

He didn't answer. He had what looked like a great life on the surface with a career, wife, and kids. But there was a piece of him still carrying so much sadness, pain, and anger. During the retreat, however, as we continued to allow for opportunities to let the truth emerge and release emotional blocks, he slowly began to see the futility of holding on to 30-year-old pain that was not serving his best interests anymore. He began to practice forgiveness, slowly but surely, for he was learning that the absence of forgiveness obstructs your access to happiness because you are constantly occupied with thoughts of that "thing" or "person" you have not forgiven. In a sense, then, forgiveness is the giver of freedom.

Commentary

In my experience, the absence of forgiveness holds us back from accessing peace and healing for ourselves. Not forgiving doesn't punish or affect those outside of us; it affects *us*. It keeps us from living fully and freely. It holds us back like an invisible umbilical cord still feeding us with what we perceive are *real* data, facts, and impressions about the older version of ourselves. This false, hurting self holds us back from experiencing the possibilities made available through a new way of being, living, seeing, thinking, and feeling. When the past hurt, anger, pain, sadness, and shame can be released and forgiven, what is left is a clearing—an open space—from which a whole new experience of life can emerge. This is living *with possibility*—a life of setbacks transformed.

Forgiveness is not a switch we can flick on in ourselves, but it can happen instantaneously, transforming the very foundation of our beliefs, if we allow it. Forgiveness does not mean we condone what someone did, letting them off the hook scot-free; it is a gift we give ourselves so that we may live our life to the fullest potential. By ending our suffering, we allow ourselves to bloom into the fully expressed life that we were meant to live rather than allow the bitterness of anger and resentment to kill every possibility of aliveness.

I have observed, in myself and in others, that denial accustoms us to a numb self, a kind of nonfeeling state in which we are blocked to pain, anger, or emotion; we live a cold, hard existence. We don't realize the burden of such an existence or the price we pay to maintain the numbness, but it is a caustic milieu brewing dark thoughts and recipes for self-destruction invisible to us. When we allow numbness to persist, we grow numb to *all* of life, not just the pain or anger we so desperately want to deny. Every now and again a glimpse of our reflection, a quiet pause, a moment of self-introspection, will hint at a foreign yet familiar stirring within. Yet we quickly retreat back to the safe shores of our comfort zone that resides in denial, knowing not to risk the danger of unraveling the truth.

Sometimes being in a state of denial delivers a pause—a much needed respite from the anguish and explosion of the pain and suffering. There is nothing wrong in that. And, in order to keep moving toward restoring our wholeness, the energy of healing needs to flow; steps toward emotional freedom from the past need to be taken. There is a fine line, a delicate balance between enjoying the rests and the notes in the music. The rests are needed, but if the denial overpowers our sense of truth, it delays the healing process and ultimately one's highest good. So while it is OK to not be OK for a time, delaying or overcoming your denial (and making a series of excuses to do so) also delays all the possibilities and opportunities for healing.

Occasionally we resist self-healing because we need proof that the abuser, the wrongdoer in our lives, has atoned for his/her sins. Some abuse victims are

(Continued on page 30)

Commentary (continued from page 29)

waiting for the day of reckoning when all wrongs will be set right. Then, only then, will it seem fair to release the past, heal old wounds, and consider the possibility of forgiveness. However, to me, forgiveness is an invitation to acknowledge your wounds and then release the burden off your soul. Once free, you can truly see within yourself that beneath all the layers of old stories and baggage, there is a deep yearning to love and be loved. Forgiveness holds compassion in the palms of its hands and makes the once hard and tough experience of life a softer, gentler one. Eventually, there is no greater joy than coming home to the heart and finding it a welcoming space filled with peace.

In a phrase often misattributed to Mark Twain, "Denial ain't just a river in Egypt." It is a river that snakes through us and can blind us with its poison. Because of it, we fail to see the truth in the present moment. But all we have is the present moment. Everything we need to know or will ever need to know is here and now. Carrying the past in our hearts or worrying about the future takes us away from enjoying the gifts of the present.

Questions for Self-Introspection

Are there things from your past that you don't like to talk about?

Are there experiences from your past that evoke fear, anger, rage, sadness, or another emotional response?

Are there people, places, movies, music, or functions that you avoid at all cost?

Who are the people you consistently shut out of your life?

What feelings do you most try to avoid?

3

New Delhi . . . and Beyond

I dropped out of school after my first year, and I moved to New Delhi, India's national capital, in June of 1992. This was a bold thing for an Indian girl in the early 1990s to do; leaving one's parents' home before marriage was looked upon with curiosity, but I was beyond caring.

In New Delhi, with my mother's help, I got an interview with a theater repertory company and got my first salaried job as an actress for 2000 rupees (rs.) a month, the equivalent of $50. I rented a small room above a garage in Defense Colony, South Delhi, an upper-middle-class part of town. My rent alone was rs. 1500 a month and with the remaining 500 I managed my groceries and bus fare. I cooked and cleaned for myself. I had been raised in an environment with domestic help provided by maids, cooks, and chauffeurs my entire life, but despite the sudden absence of all these conveniences, the air I now breathed was lighter. No one made my bed for me every morning, set the table and served every meal, or provided tea and snacks in between. No one washed, ironed, and put away my clothes, or neatly organized them in my closet. The so-called privileges and comforts of that old life seemed more like a curse. I felt free, released and blessed to do my own laundry, cooking, cleaning, and scrubbing. This was my kingdom!

In the beginning, I loved every second of it. I enjoyed a feeling of weightlessness for the first time in a long time. I stayed under budget, accounting for every *paisa* (Indian currency for one cent) I spent. Every night I would journal how much the bus ride, lunch, groceries, or anything extra cost. By keeping a close tab on my expenses, I wanted to make sure I lived within my means and never needed to ask for any money from home.

Upon waking in the mornings, I would make my breakfast while listening to *Sgt. Pepper's Lonely Hearts Club Band*, a cassette tape of a popular Beatles' album my older brother Sourabh had given me. To get music on tape during the '80s and '90s, we had to buy a pack of blank cassette tapes and take them to the music store where employees would make our custom tapes from the lists we gave them. Sourabh was really good at getting this done, and the store's owner Ruben had become a good friend by then. Sourabh had many tapes made for me that I'd listen to while making and packing my lunch, which involved cooking a vegetable from scratch and rolling out the Indian flat bread known as roti. It was never as simple as sticking a slice of ham and cheese between two pieces of bread. I never even knew I had that option! Then I'd make my bed, priding myself on leaving my loft spotless.

When I walked to the bus stop, men sexually harassed me, following and stalking me, and groping my body, especially on public transportation. Repeatedly. In India, this was called "Eve-teasing." They stalked me along the way, so sometimes I'd hop on a three-wheeled scooter taxi called an auto rickshaw, or I'd turn into a different street to try to dodge the skulkers who would follow me. Even though I was in what was considered a safe neighborhood, these shady characters were lurking at most street corners. After a 45-minute bus ride to the theater district in the central part of New Delhi called Mandi House, I'd walk the rest of the way to work where I'd meet up with friends and colleagues for a cup of chai — in the traditional sense, the omnipresent hot tea served throughout India.

I loved this part of New Delhi. Mandi House was and still is the vortex of Indian culture. Music, dance, theater, and galleries were everywhere. At every café, restaurant, and corner tea shack, I would run into dance or acting students, musicians, playwrights, and singers. It was so rich with both visual and performing arts. After spending the day attending dance lessons and working at the theater company, I'd walk to the bus stop and catch the bus back to my loft. I'd make myself some dinner and read, listen to music and sing, and rehearse my lines.

But over time this routine began to get very monotonous and lonely. This new life, and the miles that separated me from my old home, began to have a positive impact on me, but I had not anticipated the degree of my loneliness. Since I was not in a typical college or university setting, I did not see too many people who were around my age, 19. Everyone seemed to be at least five to 10 years my senior. Moreover, I was still deeply sad and very angry, missing the parts of my old life that included my brothers, my friends, and the familiarity of the town where I grew up. Missing having someone to talk to, I named my cassette player and toaster Teepo and Toto, respectively. They were the friends I spoke to at home, telling them about my day, what I was going to pack for my lunch, how I was feeling, and who said and did what at work. I didn't for a moment question the sanity of this practice.

I had enrolled in a dance program at the Sriram Bhartiya Kala Kendra, also known as SBKK, the most prestigious dance institute in the nation's capital, where hundreds of boys, girls, men, and women came from all over the world to study the performing arts. As long as the music was playing and I was dancing, I felt expressive and connected to an unstoppable energy force, feeling in control over everything in life, but the moment the music stopped, that ecstasy ended and I found I didn't know how to relate to the other students. I was socially awkward, and I had not expected that my abuse would have implications for my behavior out among other people. Now, from the perspective of experience, I have a better understanding of the various behavioral adaptations abused people make, such as overachieving, becoming antisocial or overly friendly, or isolating, and I have such compassion for that 19-year-old version of me.

Eventually I realized I needed to make some real friends, so I started opening up at work. I interacted more often with the same group of people and was getting invited to parties, events, and shows. I developed new friendships and started building community. I *never* disclosed the real reason why I had moved to New Delhi in the first place. Everyone believed it was to advance my studies in the performing arts, specifically my training in theater as an actress, and I did not tell them otherwise.

While I was in New Delhi, my younger brother, whom I still had not told of my abuse, was accepted on a scholarship to a high school in Wales called the United World College of the Atlantic that brought together students from all over the world. This was a great opportunity, and I encouraged him to take it, to get away to experience a new life. So he left for the UK and would complete his last two years of high school away from home.

I've always found it ironic that when I was in the sixth grade, my parents had been offered an opportunity to send my older brother and me to the very prestigious Doon School, a private boarding academy located in Darjeeling in the mountains of Northern India. They chose not to send us because, if we went away, our younger brother would be left alone without his siblings. Now, he was the one leaving to study abroad while we stayed in India. I was thrilled, over the moon for him, and I celebrated his freedom.

Making international or long-distance calls was not often affordable on my limited budget, at least not frequently, but occasionally I would call him when I had enough money. To balance out the infrequent calls, we wrote each other long letters to stay connected. I used to miss my brothers terribly; not having them closer to me was very depressing.

Sometimes Sourabh would come visit me in New Delhi. He loved playing the guitar and singing, and he's always had a lovely voice. He would sing Cat Stevens' "Wild World" at the end of every one of our visits. Now, whenever I hear the chorus—"Hey, baby, baby, it's a wild world / It's hard to get by, just upon a smile, girl"—it brings me back to how it felt to visit with Sourabh. It warms me still to know that singing this song was his way of giving me courage, strength, and hope in the best way he knew how. Despite the distance between us or, in Sourabh's case, the struggle to share his feelings about our secret bond, both of my brothers found their way to express their love for me.

Nevertheless, I was in such a fog during my time in New Delhi, trying to create a new world for myself, some semblance of a renewed, not-so-fractured life. I hoped that fixing my life on the outside would make me feel better about myself on the inside. I now call this period when I moved out of my parents' house my "crisis management" phase to reflect the period in which I had merely transplanted myself.

On some level, I suppose that both my parents and I assumed that this move was all that we needed to start a new chapter in all of our lives. Everyone could start to move on now, start afresh. None of us had even the slightest inkling that this respite would be temporary, or that one day the skeletons in our closets would emerge, demanding attention and forcing us to take a deliberate pause to confront our past. But for now we were in survival mode, and I was getting by day after day with simple goals like learning my lines, getting to rehearsal on time, and buying milk on the way home. Thinking about the meaning of my life, who I was, why I was who I was, and how I felt about it were not priorities or even remote possibilities for me. I had no desire for healing from, releasing, or letting go of the past. The baggage of anger and shame was still packed and sitting in a dark corner. I was unaware that although I thought I was reconstructing my life, I was building it on an unstable foundation, adding layers year after year, unaware that such flimsiness could not support their added weight for long.

As time passed, Sourabh married his sweetheart, a talented young lady he had met when he was 17. A few years later, my younger brother moved to the United States for his undergraduate studies at Middlebury College in Vermont. During his four years there, I had moved around, so soon we were all living on separate continents: I in Europe, my younger brother in the U.S., and Sourabh still back home in India. Our life as siblings in our parents' home had come to a premature and painful halt. At the time, I don't think any of us realized it. Thankfully, we remain extremely close to this day.

Experiencing the trauma of abuse as a child definitely resulted in losses across multiple areas of my life. It not only left a void with my father, my mother, and my siblings, but it also made me feel like I had experienced a time warp during my childhood. I had a sense of an erratic flow of consciousness, emotional instability, and loss of self-control. My frozen response to the trauma—that is, as long as I remained unhealed and continued to feel threatened—kept me from being present in every area of my life except the past, which I continually planted and replanted into my future.

It was during my theater phase in New Delhi that I met Sid, the man I would marry on January 19, 1995, when I was 21. We met during a theater production, just like my parents had. I thought it was "meant to be" and so did they. My mother had a friend in New Delhi who had heard stories about Sid, calling him a Cowboy Casanova—in other words, flirtatious, untrustworthy, and not the right choice as a husband for me. She tried dissuading my mother, but Mother was convinced that this was the right move and the best way for me to move on with my life, for our big *happy* family to *look* good again, with everyone doing well, everyone thriving.

At first Sid and I were just friends and colleagues rehearsing for a play together. I took my theater classes very seriously, was extremely focused, and worked really hard. He respected my talent and told me later what caught his attention was that one day, while he was mindlessly humming "Riders on the Storm" by Jim Morrison of The Doors, I chimed in and sang the second line. He did not expect music of the rock genre to come out of my mouth because I had kept the fun part of myself hidden and was just beginning to come out of my shell.

Sid was like my father in many ways. He was an engineer, had a real job during the day in sales, and had such a passion for theater that he would make time for rehearsals at night. He was also a big flirt, and I don't think he really ever wanted to be in a committed relationship. I, in turn, had very low expectations for where it would go; I didn't believe I deserved to be respected or that there could be any chance of my settling down if I didn't do it right away, while I had this chance. Having married me under pressure from his parents, who at first adored me, I think Sid wanted to get out of our relationship many times, but I was so immature that I refused to see it and instead went on to marry him.

After the wedding I didn't want to do any more acting. I wanted to be a good wife and daughter-in-law to Sid's aging parents to experience what it would be like to have a normal life in a family again. We had a joint living arrangement with his mother, father, and younger brother. I enjoyed the cooking, cleaning, and, especially, preparing welcoming dinners for him upon his return from work. I was the picture-perfect version of the good wife as depicted in images from the 1950s shown in *Good Housekeeping* magazine. I actually enjoyed this fairy-tale version of myself and found these activities very grounding. Once again, I had found a way of feeling centered in a family, in my home. I could give and receive love from Sid's father and momentarily be free of old baggage filled with the detritus of a dysfunctional father-daughter relationship. I could serve and support his parents without reminders of my past tormenting me.

But marriage didn't deter Sid from his flirtations and he had many female friends. On our honeymoon I found a picture of a model, later turned actress, in the outside pocket of his bag. I asked him about it and he said she had given it to him to give to another producer. Many months later, rumors about them appeared in magazines and papers. Within months of being married, Sid and I were drifting apart. He was distancing himself. Suddenly he had events he had to attend after hours that didn't involve me. He didn't like to bring me to parties with him. I stayed home in the background, not imposing on him, but I couldn't help but wonder how, within the first few months of being married, he would not want to be seen with me in public.

At the time I believed I knew why. *I'm not good enough. I'm damaged, broken, and dirty. This is entirely my fault, my karma. He is right for not wanting me. Who would?* We started arguing, and in one such argument he told me I disgusted him. He resented the fact that I missed him when he was gone, that he was the center of my universe, and that I couldn't wait for him to come home in the evenings. All these things, expressions of my love that I thought would endear me to him, repulsed him. Although this hurt me, I was nevertheless convinced, immediately, that his loathing me was not unwarranted. I already disgusted and repulsed myself, so it made sense that he felt the same way.

Eventually I learned that he cheated on me throughout the time we dated and during our marriage. But at the time, I did not understand that his emotions and attitude toward me were his way of justifying his adulterous behavior and actions. Fearful that I would come to deny Sid's dysfunctional behavior just as my mother had denied my father's, I kept telling myself, *I will not turn into my mother, I will not turn into my mother.* Repeating this phrase served as my wake-up call. I had to get my life straightened out.

I decided I did not want to rely on Sid anymore. He had humiliated me, and I wanted to get back to being self-sufficient, which meant getting back out in society and reconnecting with my acting network. It meant going to events of my own, looking after my fitness and wellness, and putting myself back into my life. I needed to look for work and have my own income stream, a livelihood.

So I engaged in a diet and exercise program, getting into great shape. Then I approached Rakesh Shreshtha, one of the best, most expensive, and hard-to-get-hold-of portrait photographers in Bombay, who agreed to take glamour shots of me.

The early '90s were watershed years in the Indian television industry. Cable television had just opened up avenues for private companies to create and launch TV channels, not just shows. India was going the way of the Western world. No longer did we have just the two TV stations I had known all my life—the National TV Channel and a statewide TV station. Now we had BBC, Zee TV, and Star TV, with new TV stations coming up every day. The industry was booming, and I was right there at the beginning when everyone was figuring it out, making tons of pilots and trying new and different styles and forms of creative expression. With the plethora of opportunities in the industry, a decent set of acting skills, and my new glam shots, I soon had both TV and commercial offers coming in.

My new career ventures would start with a phone call to come to an audition. If the audition went well, there would be a callback and then a meeting with the producer and director. If I passed muster, I would then usually meet with the production manager to talk about money and see if the calendar had openings for shooting dates. The next steps involved my getting into costume and making arrangements for hair and makeup.

One by one, auditions, pilots, and projects started coming my way. Slowly but surely, the money also started coming in. Sid and I were both leading busy lives working in television. At times I would arrive at an audition and find him there. He had a car and I did not, so I used public transport. When I asked him why he didn't tell me he was going to the same audition, as we could have driven together, he would make up some flaky excuse. And I, wanting to avoid conflict, would just let it pass. One time when I ran into him at an audition and asked if I could drive back with him, he said no. Apparently he had to go somewhere else and needed to leave right away, so he claimed he could not wait until my audition was done. I remember carrying a small umbrella with me since there were heavy thunderstorms that day.

Because of our exposure in the Bombay television and film industry during the mid-1990s, Sid and I both would occasionally appear in the local press and media. Every so often, however, there would be news about him with other women—mainly one woman, the one from the picture on our honeymoon—over and over again. But I denied any of the rumors. *These can't be true. The press makes stuff up all the time.*

But one day when I returned from a weeklong film shoot and the security guard welcomed me at my apartment building, I asked him if everything had been going well in my absence. He responded that yes, it had, and that my sister had been visiting often.

My sister? I didn't have one.

That was the day I knew that Sid and I were done, it was over, he had to go. By then, we had our own place. Enraged, I went upstairs and threw out all his clothes, emptied his perfume bottles, and took a pair of scissors to his suits. When he came home that night from his parents' place, drunk, I told him he could stay the night, pass out for all I care, but in the morning I wanted him gone. I had even found a piece of jewelry in the bathroom left behind after his rendezvous in our apartment. *My home.* He has brought another woman into my *home.* I was infuriated.

In a dramatic fit, he smashed his head through the china cabinet, giving himself a big gash on his head. I coldly watched the blood starting to stream down his face.

"Don't make me leave, please don't do this. I love you so much. I'm sorry," he pleaded. I felt like stone, a lifeless statue. Even though I was boiling mad on the inside, I remained expressionless, almost stoic, on the outside. Even glad that he was hurt. I had seen enough, tried enough, and I was determined I would not turn into my mother.

When he saw that I wouldn't budge, he said, "Let's have a baby; everything will work itself out."

That's when I got even more determined. There was no way I was going to let him father any baby I was going to bring into this world.

Within a day, news of our separation was the headline in the entertainment section of the *Times of India* newspaper, and his family started calling me. I didn't deny the news. I knew it was over. His mother informed me that she wanted our cordless phone back because they had bought it. She said that it would be okay if I kept one of two stainless steel armoires, but they wanted the other one back. I could have cared less about the stupid phone and armoire! I just wanted my life back. It seemed like I had worked so hard to re-establish it, and once again it had turned to rubbish.

So Sid and I separated, and I dove fully back into my acting career. I was up for anything. All I had to do was show up on set, apply makeup, rehearse my lines, and LIGHTS! CAMERA! ACTION! I was on point every time, playing role after role without any hesitation. After all, it was easier pretending to be someone other than myself. I could escape the pain of being me, of expressing my own life, living my own truths.

This busy, glitzy, glamorous, yet mostly phony part of my journey gave me space in which to buffer myself from the real world, real people, real feeling, and real relationships. I isolated myself, claiming a haven of solitude where I could try to heal from the wounds of the battles that had been my life. I didn't feel like I was winning, but I knew I could fight enough to get by for another day. Speaking the unspeakable was never even a consideration, nonnegotiable.

Eventually, however, I found I needed a break, some sort of respite from self-loathing. I took a short trip to an ashram by the ocean in Pondicherry with my older brother. It was a long weekend for us, and he and I drove quietly, spending the days in calm reflection by the waves of the sea with an occasional beer and delicious Indian fried fish. My brother gave me the space to breathe, think, and just be. It was in this pause without distractions that I became able to look at the me who I was pretending to be. I discovered that by stepping back from the drama and upheaval that was in my past, I was able to view the movie of my own life as objectively as any anonymous member of an audience.

I remember being both disappointed as I watched my life play out in front of me and calmly detached at the same time. *This was me, but this was also not me. This is what happened, but this was not everything.* My inner dialog veered from caustic to philosophical. Existential questions— *Who am I? How am I feeling about my past? What do I want from my life?*—arose occasionally and I found myself okay with these interludes. They didn't confuse me like they had or create more turmoil. Some insights floated though. I didn't always like that, as they opened new doors and gave birth to new questions, so I often stepped back, not always enjoying this newly developing self-discovery and awareness.

But even in my resistance, I appreciated that I was at least having a conversation with myself. It was awkward, but it finally felt like I was meeting a part of me that was untouched by what had happened to me. Although I didn't like the person I saw in my own personal movie, I became intrigued by this new self-awareness that made me hopeful it could precipitate some fortuitous reversals in my life.

One day I would feel optimistic and the next day depressed, directionless. At such times, I was very irritable and unconcerned about my acting success or failure. I was inconsistent and unfocused—almost uncaring whether I had a job or not—like I was in a fog. I was just living one day at a time. I drank and smoked with my artist friends, writers, and producers, convinced there was no hope for me, no feeling better about myself. While others thought I had it all—the cars, the entourage, the Gucci sunglasses—I was miserable and, at one of the most glamorous times of my life, I felt completely unattractive.

In the middle of all this disorder and disruption, I got a call from my father asking if I would be willing to speak with someone with whom he had just studied healing. While I was in New Delhi and not on talking terms with him, he had been seeking to understand himself, to heal and transform. I did not know about any of this at the time as we never spoke, and my mother and brother did not discuss his activities with me. The healing modality he referred to was Reiki. I instantly dismissed his suggestion, angry that he, of all people, had the audacity to suggest that I needed healing. *Who did he think he was? How dare he? To hell with him!* I told him to leave me alone.

A few months later, a filmmaker friend of mine was preparing to shoot a panel discussion for a television show on the latest healing techniques that were gaining popularity the world over. One of these was Reiki, which he found particularly interesting. I paused, remembering the call from my father. A week later, a newspaper ad caught my eye that mentioned a weekend class teaching Reiki as a natural, therapeutic technique. Finally, I called the number in the ad and signed up for the class. By now, whatever this Reiki was had my attention. I hoped that something good might come out of it, but I never really admitted it aloud as I did not want to be disappointed like I was in college.

I showed up in quite a cynical and arrogant frame of mind, almost as though I wanted to prove that such therapies were full of nonsense. I talked myself into sitting through the two-day seminar with the "losers" who'd attended, and I left the class on Sunday night quite underwhelmed, not in the least convinced that there was any value in what they were claiming to be the "subliminal healing effects of Reiki." Nevertheless, my resistance to the other participants had eased, and I'd even developed a slight connection to the Reiki teacher. So I concluded that the weekend had been an interesting experiment that I would file away and never think about again.

A few months later, I noticed that the severe sinusitis that had plagued me since I was 14 had vanished. For as long as I could recall, my allergies to dust, incense, and firewood smoke caused me to sneeze for days, completely incapacitating me. I would have to stay home, feeling miserable with boxes of tissue and a wastepaper basket by my side. But now, suddenly, I was no longer reacting to others' perfume or burning incense.

Subsequently, I began to notice that, despite our separation, the toxicity of my relationship with Sid was easing as we embarked on a mutually agreed-upon divorce. New, healthy relationships began entering my life. Friends who made me feel good about myself were becoming part of my world, and that helped me find and maintain a more positive outlook. I found myself laughing more and feeling a renewed sense of lightness. Was all this a coincidence? First the allergies, then improved relationships?

During this same period, I appeared in a movie requiring that I dance. But over the years, I had developed severe corns on my feet that had become so painful by this time I could barely walk. So I would wrap my feet in bandages and try all kinds of homemade remedies to try to heal the corns and alleviate the pain. None of them had worked.

I was on location in the mountains filming a song-and-dance sequence for the movie, and with my discomfort becoming unbearable, I turned to Louise Hay's *Heal Your Body*, a book in which she shares a list she has curated over her years of interpreting the metaphysical meanings of physical symptoms. When I looked up "corns," I found that she believes they are a manifestation of "hardened areas of thought—stubborn holding on to the pain of the past." I clearly remember how it hit me in a split second as I connected the dots: I still had a laundry list of complaints with my past relationships, thoughts, and expectations that I held close. The author recommended this affirmation: "I surrender to the Universe and let myself move forward 'freely.'"

I felt it in a flash, the surreal experience of becoming unburdened from physical and emotional obstacles, one by one, and I was suffused with a feeling of well-being as though my body's innate ability to heal itself had suddenly awakened. The next morning after I got out of bed, in fact, I found I wasn't walking on the outer edges of my feet—I could actually place them directly on the floor. There was no pain. How was this possible? I can't deny it happened, however; I remember the exact day and place. I was amazed, truly amazed. Although I'd initially been full of resistance with a healthy dose of cynicism toward Reiki, things were shifting within me since I'd taken that class.

Then one day, my father's Reiki teacher called and I answered the phone. We had a brief conversation, and it so happened that there was a weekend intensive course she was leading that weekend in a different city. Aware of my separation, something she learned from my father, she asked if I would join them. Apparently my father would also be her assistant.

I was not pleased that I would have to travel somewhere to participate in a retreat among strangers, nor was I looking forward to an extended weekend with my father lurking around, a witness to my participation. I was deeply conflicted about the whole weekend and really unhappy to be in the car with him for four hours going to something I was not even interested in. Or so I told one part of myself. But another part of me had said yes. Nobody was forcing me to go. Something inside of me must have agreed to have this experience, even though I did not trust my inner voice. *See where it had landed me to begin with? How could I trust it?*

The four-hour drive went by without a word spoken between us. Not only that, I don't even recall my father being at the intensive class the entire weekend—it's as though that memory was erased. I remember the retreat, the work, my transformation, the exercises, meditations, and participants, but for quite some time, any memory of my father's presence was gone.

Initially, my usual defenses kicked in; I gave everyone at the retreat the impression that I was indifferent to all of them. *I, the actress, shall have nothing to do with you.* I had already been in several primetime TV shows, a major soap opera, and three full-length features. I was accustomed to signing autographs at airports and shopping malls. I had shows on TV as well as movies that were running in the theaters and thus was easily recognized, so I used my actressy glamour to hide the scared little girl who lurked within, someone who just wanted to have friends and be loved. Yet I avoided having to mingle with others by engrossing myself in reading the novels I had brought. I never looked up or made eye contact with any of the participants because I was afraid I would have to speak to them if I did.

It was at the end of the first day when Prema, the seminar leader, walked up to me with her entourage of assistants. I was sitting on the floor of the seminar room leaning up against a pillar, totally committed to finishing one of John Grisham's best-selling novels. I looked up at her as she spoke.

"Hi . . ."

"Hi," I said, surprised to see four people standing there towering above me.

"What are you reading?" she asked.

I rolled my eyes, quite frustrated that I was being interrupted. *Isn't it obvious that I should really be left alone?* But I stifled that voice and instead extended my arm out to show her the cover of the book. She looked at it, took it in her hand, turned around, and walked away.

I watched, stunned, as the group of individuals walked away from me. I quickly looked around to check to see if anyone had witnessed my humiliation. *There was no way she just did that. No way. Did she? Really?*

I was pissed, really pissed, but I had nowhere to go with that anger other than stuff it down inside—along with my pride.

The next day, we had an early morning meditation; the first 20 minutes involved intense breathing designed to help shake up one's energy that resides in deeply buried emotions, followed by primal screaming.

At first, when the instructions for the meditation were given, there were some uncomfortable giggles and chuckles from some of the participants.

"Scream? Ha, that's funny. I have nothing to be mad at; my life is good," were some of the participants' initial reactions. But 15–20 minutes into the meditation when the catharsis phase begins—it can look different to each participant—someone may scream, laugh, dance, or stand still. The point is to participate fully for the therapeutic experience that this meditation, rightfully called "dynamic" meditation, has to offer. The meditation was created by Osho, formerly known as Rajneesh. I now use this and several other meditations of his during my retreats.

Others who were at this retreat in 1997 say they still remember me—not because I was "the actress" but because I was the loudest and most profane participant during this meditation. I gave it my 100 percent, my 200 percent—not actually possible, of course, but I did not hold back. What Prema had done the previous night had made me confront something that I had not been able to do on my own. She made me confront me.

For the first time, I had been stripped of the veil I had been so delicately holding in place. For the first time ever someone had so boldly commanded that I BE WHO I AM—speak my truth and express, really authentically express, how I truly felt. I was led by Prema in this meditation to just let go, to say the words I wanted to say—and not hold back!

I screamed, I yelled, I shouted out all the words, the anger, the abuses that I had wanted to express outwardly to my father. I had even forgotten that he was right there. *You bastard, you son of a bitch, how could you—I was just a little girl! I hate you!*

This was the first moment in my life I was looking inside of me—I was face to face with the traumatized self that I was: angry, confused, ashamed, and, above all, sad—very, very sad. The initial primal scream-ing helped break the barriers and stirred the real emotions inside. Sud-denly it felt like I had discovered a whole new universe of untapped emo-tions within me.

Until that moment, I had never been given—given myself—permis-sion to fully express what I was feeling. I had been trained to do the opposite. I had been trained to keep the secret. *Never tell anyone. This has to die with me.* I had never imagined that a day would come when I could experience even the slightest release, that I would realize there was a light at the end of the tunnel. I could see it—it was within me. I had it in me to reach for that light.

During the rest of the seminar, I was the most enthusiastic partici-pant. I was the first to volunteer for the demonstrations of the exercises. I turned into this bright-eyed and bushy-tailed student. No ego, arro-gance, or casting myself off into my ivory tower of isolation. My walls had come down. I was so humbled by this experience. I not only made eye contact with the other attendees, but I hugged everyone, danced, and had the best time of my life.

This was a hairpin turn into the first ray of light on my journey when I had almost been consumed by the darkness. I clung to this ray of light and, one inch at a time, I moved forward into it where I began to find myself. With awareness, healing, and energy, my transformation, layer by layer, had begun.

One evening at the end of my retreat with Prema, we were just relax-ing with a few other participants and team members, and she asked me about the Reiki class I had taken. Good-naturedly, she quizzed me on some basic information about Reiki that I should have known if I had really been listening at the time instead of being there only to refute the notion that Reiki actually worked.

It became clear during our discussion that I needed to take the first level of Reiki again and really pay attention this time around. If it had had so many positive effects on me when I had not really been paying attention, too busy resisting and belittling the whole experience, I could only imagine what taking it seriously might do. So I signed up, with Prema this time. Later on, she initiated me into all three levels of Reiki, and on May 5, 2002, I became a Reiki master and teacher in the tradi-tional Usui method of Reiki healing.

I was still working in film and TV and had an entourage with a hairstylist, make-up artist, personal assistant, and chauffeur as well as my own wardrobe designer. Everywhere I went, my staff went with me. All I had to do was sit in my chair, and they got to work getting me ready for my next shot in front of the camera.

A regional TV show I did in South India really took off, and I started getting a lot of offers from the booming South Indian film and TV industry. During this time I had been participating in more Reiki classes and advanced workshops for self-healing. I had also attended a few additional intensive seminars and been training closely with Prema, and that really helped me with forgiveness and self-expression. Slowly but surely my relationship with my parents was improving; we were communicating. My visits to their home started increasing, and I began catching up on lost time and visiting with them more. After the divorce, I didn't want to live by myself immediately, so I donated my belongings in Bombay and moved back to the family home, making that my primary home base. With what felt like a blank slate, I was once again ready to launch my life.

I had always loved dogs and had wanted one since I was a little girl, but my parents never allowed it for fear of the responsibility. Right after my separation from Sid, I decided not to get into any relationships and just focus on my healing, and that's when I decided a dog would be the most reliable companion to have around. So I made up my mind—I was getting a dog, and I discussed this idea with my parents.

"It's either me or a dog in this house," my father threatened, but little did he know that his comment actually made my decision easier for me. I brought home six-week-old Hobbit the same day. He was one of six Lhasa Apsos in the litter, and as soon as our eyes met, it was love at first sight. My father, despite initial resistance, was smitten too. Within five minutes of Hobbit's arrival at the house, I was shocked to see him kneeling on the floor trying to feed the puppy milk from a baby cup. My father! He might have threatened me in the beginning, but he was also quite a sentimental and soppy guy.

I ended up having to leave for Paris at the end of 1998, the same year I got my sweet dog. Although he lived with me in Paris for a brief period of time, he ended up becoming not my best friend and companion but my father's. And so he remained for the 15 years that followed until little Hobbit from Hobbiton left us for doggie heaven. I believe he provided my father with many moments of joy, healing, and transformation, as he was someone my father cherished. Sometimes I think my only role was to bring them together as they were practically soul mates. But Hobbit had also taught me how to be open to the possibility of receiving unconditional love, and being open was healing for me. It allowed for a positive outlook toward my life that had the ripple effect of allowing me to see the serendipity, beauty, and grace in the world, to listen more attentively, and to share and be present with others—especially those who were really important to me.

Hobbit helped me find ways to access happiness and to experience a loving connection without apprehension. I had forgotten what that felt like. He created room in my life for joy, laughter, and pure, innocent fun. We had a signature tune for when it was time for his bath and brushing his lovely Lhasa Apso locks. All I had to do was start singing; he knew what would be coming next.

Although Hobbit isn't here anymore, he is a testament to the possibilities that lie within us to heal. Our transformation can be accomplished any time, any place, and with any body—human or not. Horses, dogs, cats, and several other types of pets have been known to facilitate healing in many people's lives.

Here's to you, my sweet Hobbit! I see you chasing butterflies and running freely all over green pastures beyond the rainbow. I miss you and you will always live in my heart. Thank you for the difference you made in my life.

☙

On my way to Europe, I also decided to visit with family in England as well as travel all over the continent. Then, in Paris at 25 years old, I found myself in a relationship with a man 10 years older than me. It seemed so right at first. *This is it—he must be the one. Why else did I go through all that I went through? It was so I could move to Paris and have this wonderfully artistic lifestyle in France! What more could I want? Sipping wine, sitting on the terraces in the cafés on the street, speaking French. This is perfect!*

Although Paris was simply inspiring, the relationship was not healthy, and it began to drain me emotionally and mentally. I found myself writing and painting like I had never before, partly because that's how my new lover could keep track of me; if I was out of his sight, he feared that I was seeing someone else.

I gradually went from writing romantic poetry to dwelling on misery, loss, and betrayal. In my paintings, I was depicting Indian women with the vermillion in their hair and on their foreheads turning into suffering females with bleeding, weeping eyes. These figures were disproportionate in size, having long arms as if they were reaching for something—help, maybe? There was one of the back of an Indian woman in a sari walking on a yellow brick road like Dorothy in *The Wizard of Oz*. Trying to find her way home, perhaps? Although I had Reiki, meditation, and transformation training, the situation in Paris still got the better of me.

Looking back, I can see that sporadic sessions of Reiki or a few weekend transformation retreats did not provide a permanent cure. Transformation is a lifelong process, a journey of healing. One has to continue to practice the work outside of classes and workshops. The opportunities for profound transformation are right here and now, in our everyday lives, not in some far-off, distant place. The practice is to be present to them when they appear.

I learned that just the one transformational weekend experience of '97 was not going to permanently heal me from over a decade of abuse and psychological wounding. It gave me a great start, but without a consistent process to follow up with that initial burst of transformation, the intense rush of joy slowly began to fade and the old voices in my head began to reappear. I realized then that there is no such thing as a drive-through breakthrough—nor is enlightenment available in a to-go cup. I had to stay the course, continue to work on myself—that is what I *could* do about where I found myself now. There were no shortcuts. I had to get *fully* present to the disorder I had drawn back into my life—despite the Reiki, meditation, and transformation. In order to create a lasting sense of peace, wholeness, and balance I had to make radical shifts in my thinking, behaviors, words, and actions. I had to step through, not over, my mess and step up to raise my self-awareness.

As a spiritual teacher and transformation leader, this has been one of the biggest lessons learned. In order to be empowered as a teacher and leader one needs to commit to being a student with a lifelong love of learning. I don't think one ever stops learning on this journey. I have been answering the same questions from homework I received in 1996, and I find that every few years when I reflect on these questions, new insights appear. Although self-help books do offer poignant guidance, I believe that one's greatest learning comes from within. But in order to do so you need to slow down, get present, and pause to understand your-self—closing your two eyes and opening them on the inside to really see and meet yourself.

I tell my clients and students who are holistic practitioners, coaches, and heart-based leaders, "Leaders and healers: Heal thyself!" In order to serve our clients and students we need to not only leave no stone unturned with our own healing, but also continue to stay with the practice of con-tinued reflection, inquiry, and introspection. We are a vessel for the work of transformation. As a musician would, we need to keep our instrument in tune and our vessel empty. Only then can we serve to our fullest and highest potential.

Even in Paris, the most beautiful city in the world, I couldn't find the peace that I was seeking. In a city that is a symbol for artistic expression and freedom, I found myself trapped. Even when I moved from city to city, from relationship to relationship, I still ended up repeating the same pattern. I still felt incomplete, unhappy, disappointed, and dejected. My inner voice kept reminding me that I was unworthy, broken, damaged, and dirty. *I am getting what I deserve.* Nevertheless, I thought Paris would be the city where I spent the rest of my life.

A movie in which I had acted before moving to Paris was released. I played the leading female character in this movie and soon was being offered lead roles in India. I turned them away. I met my life and the opportunities that came my way with the same attitude with which I saw myself—I was not good enough for my life, and these roles were not good enough for me. So I kept rejecting new movie offers. I had been traveling from one country to the next, but I had still not addressed the pain that was at my core or the beliefs that I had formed about myself. I was so disconnected from myself that I don't think, even if someone with all the qualities I thought I desired had appeared in front of me, that I would have recognized it. And yet again, I found myself back at my parents' home, figuring out what I was going to do with my life.

I recommitted to my energy healing, meditation, and transformation practices and enrolled in classes that would help broaden my repertory of modalities. I began feeling less charged by emotions and was once again able to feel a renewed sense of inner calm and peace like right after my first retreat in 1997.

In 2001, after Paris, I found myself in a much more grounded, cen-tered, and mellow time in my life, and I received an email from my mother's best friend, a woman who had migrated to the United States. My mother had sent her a link to an online interview that included one of my glamour shots. The woman also sent a copy to her two children who had been childhood friends of my brothers and me. In response to that, her son Ankash, whom we called Anky when we were growing up, wrote back, and we started corresponding via emails with each other. Next thing I knew, his emails were getting longer, and there was some poetry coming my way as well. An online Yahoo chat followed, and then phone calls. We were falling for each other.

I began to freak out a little. *How can I fall for someone I only know online? Yes, I might have known him from when I was four years old, but that doesn't mean much. What if he is some horrible person now?* Especially since he was an American and we had already heard horror stories of Indian girls (my own aunt being one of them) who had married Americans, only to return battered and abused to India.

But somewhere inside I felt a calm peace when I communicated with Anky, and I wanted to keep this feeling going. Finally, after our correspondence had been going on for months, he decided he was going to come to India to see me. So on July 4, Ankash Badami, now going by Kash, landed at Chennai Airport and my heart skipped several beats. He was a gorgeous man with broad shoulders, mocha skin, beautiful brown eyes, and he simply swept me off my feet. We hadn't seen each other since we were 9 or 10, but here we were 16 years later, and he and I still remembered each other very fondly as one another's first friend.

The 12 days we spent together were incredible. We laughed, talked, danced, and spent every moment together getting to know each other as fast as we possibly could. We devoted every possible minute to sharing and tasting all the different Indian foods that we wanted—especially the desserts. On July 14, just 10 days after dating "in person," he asked my grandmother, who was living with us at the time, if he could marry me. She was surprised and thrilled! Then he asked my parents, who were over the moon with the idea. And then he asked me, and I said yes.

On July 16 when he left to go back to Washington, DC, I knew it was only a matter of time before we would be together again. I will never forget how sad he looked walking into the airport as I stood there waving, watching him leave. I spent the next six months refocusing my energy on my healing and spiritual journey. I took more classes, learning even more modalities and healing techniques. I also took a trip to the Himalayas to study pottery. I lived in a cottage with a view of the Himalayan range, whose majestic presence and spectacular views I could see when I looked up from the potting wheel. It was a lovely time during which Kash and I chose our wedding date: February 14, 2002.

RETREAT CASE

A student of mine who has participated and engaged in practically every program and product I have offered said to me the first time we met, "I have already done the work; I don't need to go back in my past any more. I am good."

"OK," I responded to her, "but still, come to the I AM Love and Aliveness Retreat. I think there's something in it for you."

She did sign up, and in the retreat's first five minutes of the opening circle, she had tears rolling down her face as she confronted all the lies she had been telling herself. When she actually paused to take an honest look within, she realized that she was not that "good." But now here she was in a sacred and safe space, given permission to explore within herself. In her own work and career, she taught people how to succeed in life and business. In her life, however, she was feeling a little lost and vulnerable. But now she was ready to dive deeper into her inner awareness to release the blocks that were holding her back. That day she began a journey in her life that even now she continues to explore as she moves forward. Her life began to transform as she took her first steps on the hairpin turn on her journey. Since the retreat, this student has written a book, launched a new business, and is an international best-selling author, coach, consultant, and entrepreneur.

Commentary

Our blocks are invisible to us. The very thing that is holding us back, the thing that we have to be free of, remains elusive for a very long time. It takes pausing, deliberate pausing, to look at ourselves to recognize that there is something inside for us to be liberated from. Far too often I hear people say,

"Oh, please don't go there!"

But I say, "Go there—please, go there," because if you don't go there, you won't go anywhere. You will stay stuck right where you are. The goal in revisiting the past is not to stir up a hornet's nest. The goal is to embrace the past, the shadows of our life trailing behind us, and being okay with that. A shadow can exist only in the light; there are no shadows in the dark. Forgiving and completing with the people, events, and experiences of our past comprise an invitation to a portal of peace. By completing, I mean expressing what there is to express, forgiving whatever there is to forgive. Resetting, coming to a place of neutral . . . not charged by strong negative emotions. Being complete with someone means to be whole, at peace with where you are in your relationship, no longer carrying the stories of your past.

Forgiving someone for what seems like something impossible to forgive is more painful than the actual experience you might be forgiving him or her for. By forgiving, you might fear you are signaling that you are okay with what they did or that you find their actions were acceptable, but forgiveness is none of that. Forgiving someone gives you the freedom to live your life with possibility again; to be free to move forward; to be alive, self-expressed, authentic, and whole in an entirely new way for yourself. We forgive because it frees us; it releases us.

No amount of trying to appear and pretend that everything is okay will allow you to live and breathe your life with authenticity. Masks, facades, and charades just take up time, and, before you know it, 20, 30, even 40 years of your life have gone by and you are exactly where you were. Dreams, longings, passions have all been thwarted. To borrow a phrase from 12-step programs, trying to "fake it till you make it" while at your core you are miserable will only help you create more of the very misery you are so accustomed to. Not fully recognizing the emotional residue from the past while trying to create a successful, happy, and whole life on the surface is like putting icing on mud pie. It just doesn't work. We must pause to recognize, release, and re-energize our lives so that we can create lasting transformation and success in all areas.

Questions for Self-Introspection

Take a moment and think about your life:

- Who are you?

- What surrounds you?

- Who are the people in your life?

- What does your world look like?

- How do you feel about all of this?

- Have you made the choices that you are living with today out of love or fear?

- Have you been able to forgive the people, events, and experiences from your past?

- How would it make you feel, think, and act to be in a reconciled and peaceful relationship with the very people from your past with whom you were once angry?

- Would you be open to reconciliation, or would you avoid it at all cost?

- How would avoiding reconciled relationships feel?

- How would healing and forgiving your old relationships feel?

Beginning to Heal

I always say to my retreat participants and students that there are many layers in the personal transformation process and they can only be present to one layer at a time. It took a long time for me to arrive at a place of equilibrium, and getting there required considerable energy and effort. It was not all smooth sailing. Just when I thought I was cruising along and the waves in the sea had leveled out, I would hit another swale. Just when I thought nothing else could go wrong, there would be an unexpected twist on my journey.

But something kept bringing me back. That first cathartic experience with Prema at the retreat and the opening that followed had given me a new perspective and a palpable sense of the potential for releasing my past and healing my pain. Even though I knew I had miles to go, I knew I could get back on track. I could do this.

Having Prema as a mentor was instrumental and kept me accountable to my continued transformation and spiritual commitments. I have had many teachers in my life, but for 16 years, partly while I was in India and then continuing after I moved to the United States, Prema always encouraged me to stay on my transformational journey and reconnect when I felt lost.

There was a deep desire within me to learn all I possibly could about how energy, in the metaphysical sense, worked. What was the energetic impact of our thoughts and beliefs? I had started reading books; taking courses, classes, and workshops; and listening to audiotapes of lectures and meditations every chance I had. Through all of my learning, it was clear that our thoughts have a profound and significant influence on our words and actions. Thoughts, words, and actions, in turn, create our belief systems, which then shape our worldview, consistently wiring and rewiring us to be who we are. So I searched out all the relevant knowledge I could find, transforming from the once-resigned and cynical student into a devoted scholar with an insatiable love of learning. It felt wonderful to have this vitality restored.

I studied several healing and energy modalities to their highest levels and participated in yearlong programs of meditation and transformation work. I began assisting Prema and traveling with her across India to teach large retreat groups. I received some of the best training from international seminar leaders and continued to absorb all the teachings, wisdom, and philosophies that crossed my path. The knowledge, inner power, and healing that were awakened in me through this work were extraordinary and created within me a sense of peace and calm.

I was committed to living an authentic life based in self-love and care. I was going to stay focused on my life's journey, heal, and serve humanity. Work as an actress continued on the side but wasn't my main focus. It helped me make a living, but when I was not shooting on set, I was assisting Prema with a seminar or traveling with her and her team for weekend retreats.

Orchid Garden with Papa

Along with all the courses and classes I was taking, I was aware that just learning the theoretical aspects of personal transformation and meditation was not going to be enough. Intellectually knowing techniques that could deliver emotional healing was inadequate; I needed to apply the theory, to practice living what I was learning in order to embody my experience. Especially now, at the threshold of starting my life over with Kash, I wanted my life to be free of anger and resentment. I didn't want to bring my past into this new life and disturb it with negative reminiscences, hurts, and thoughts. I wanted a radical shift.

I had still never confronted my father, face to face, about what had happened. The cathartic breakthrough at my first retreat enabled me to verbalize the emotions in a safe place and let out the pent-up rage, blame, and shame. Although I had built trust with a couple of participants and begun a journey of renewal, I still had not actually spoken about the abuse, its impact on me, or my feelings about it directly to my father. He was right there, in my life, and we interacted on a superficial level, pretending everything was already in the past, forgiven and complete. I had done enough transformation work and facilitated enough completion exercises with participants to know that more healing was required in my relationship with my father. (A "completion" is a very powerful exercise. It is expressing—communicating authentically—how you feel without blaming another or allowing a shame of the self. In a completion, there is no interpretation or judgment of what happened during events of the past or making the other person "wrong" for what they did. It is understanding that what happened was in the past, and that in this moment you are ready to create a new possibility for your future with this person.) This told me I needed to do what I could to move that process along and not fear it or try to escape. I was going to get married in a few months, and time was of the essence. I did not want even traces of undesirable energies entering my new life.

My intention to confront him, however, did not come from anger or blame. My resentment toward him had been transformed into forgiveness over the course of the previous five years of work at the retreats. Now I was ready to face him and ask him: "Why?"

We made a trip to Auroville Ashram, a three-hour drive by road from Madras (now called Chennai) where we lived. We had both made several individual trips to Auroville and Pondicherry (twin cities in Tamil Nadu, South India), the original town where the ashram was built. I had attended seminars as well as assisted Prema on retreats there. My father too had made several spiritual retreats to the ashram on his own. But this was our first trip together. It was a way to verify that the transformation and healing were real. We would be driving together and staying together in the same cottage for a weekend. I was ready.

Back then, the rural roads to Auroville had several encampments of huts known as hutments along either side of them. At one point we came upon a roadside arrack shop—arrack is a southern-Indian alcoholic beverage made with sugar cane and the sap of coconut flowers. As I slowed down in front of the shop, a drunken man on foot came out of nowhere and smashed into my windshield. He didn't get hurt, but suddenly what seemed like 50 angry villagers charged our car and started beating it with sticks, shattering the windshield. Inside the car, I was terrified and I regretted this entire trip, viewing it as evidence that I should never have tried to make it. *Look at what I've done now!*

My father got out of the car and asked me to lock it from inside. It just so happened that the car behind us, also on the way to Auroville, contained four men who were my father's colleagues. Along with my father, they calmed the crowds and gave the villagers some money, even though no harm had befallen the man.

For me, being recognized as a movie star in the middle of this chaos was interesting. I could hear the villagers shouting out my name as the crowd kept getting bigger and bigger. I began to feel an extra element of protection emanating from the crowd. Nevertheless, wanting to be sure everything was sorted out before continuing our trip to Auroville, my father and I, and his colleagues, ended up going to the police station to file a complaint. While waiting for my father to complete the process, I began speaking with one of my father's four acquaintances. I learned that they knew my father from Sunday morning religious meetings. *Interesting*, I thought to myself. *This is how you know him? And in this hour of crisis you all dropped out of nowhere and are here to protect me, support him, and get us out of this mess?*

We hadn't even reached the ashram yet and I felt like our journey was already a metaphor for the past 20-plus years. The chaos, the crisis, the helplessness, the fear were all mixed up and reflective of our life's journey. It was like that weekend would not have been complete without that accident. It was practically necessary to put things in perspective; for me to feel okay with my helplessness and vulnerability and to see my father in that moment as the man he once was in my life, capable of protecting me from harm. I noticed that when I saw him that way, I wasn't seeing an abuser but a father. And instead of judging myself for not hating him anymore, I felt at peace. I felt like it was okay to be in that space, felt the burden of blame lifting off of me and the weight of accusing him for what he had done become lighter. I was able to allow this awareness to flow into me because of my transformation work that released my suppressed emotions in the years leading up to this moment. Without doing that work, I don't believe I would have been equipped to have the insights I had in those moments by myself in the car. I don't think I would have responded to this situation in the calm manner that I did.

The next day, my father and I sat on the ground in an orchid garden facing each other in silence. We were embarking on an exercise we had learned through our training with Prema to facilitate completions with a sharing partner or participant. Only this time, we were not going to be *pretending* we were making a completion with a particular person, we were *actually* making it with the real person. Tears were streaming from both his eyes and mine, even before the first word was spoken.

The key to this exercise is when one participant speaks, the other just listens, without judgment or opinion, and doesn't interrupt. I took this opportunity to say what I felt in the layers that were then apparent to me. First I spoke, he listened. There was no anger, yelling, or screaming at him. I had released at the retreat all that had happened in the past, and how, for the majority of my life, I felt like all that negative emotion really just lived inside of me. Now, around three-quarters of the way into the session when it felt like all that needed to be said had been said, for the first time I spoke the following words to him: "I forgive you, I love you, thank you for all you have done for me, please forgive me for what I may have done to you." And he cried—not overtly, but just a steady stream of tears rolling down his face.

Finally, he spoke and said something similar to me, and he told me that he had been abused as a child—a revelation to me. This was a very raw moment for us. We were there as two beings birthed into this life as father and daughter trying to make sense of our relationship and examine our potential for healing ourselves as well as being there for each other. Was it even possible or was this an exercise in futility? Something within me told me it was okay to stay with the possibility of healing. I wanted it. I wanted my life to be better. I wanted to see that there was still hope in this world for all of us, that there was still a possibility for deliverance for both the abused and the abuser. I could see the anguish on both sides, the pain and suffering on both sides, and remorse on both sides for the loss of time in living life fully. I began to understand that my continuing in the role of victim only continued to add fuel to my image of him as an abuser. As long as I call myself a survivor, I continue to give energy to the fact that I may have ceased to exist in my wholeness at one point, thus keeping my sense of victimhood alive forever. I was ready to let go and release that. And so I did.

I chose to release the labels and the story and embrace the possibility of unconditional healing, forgiveness, love, and compassion. I chose to explore the possibility that while living this life and breathing this air,

I could transform and shift my thoughts, memories, and emotions so that they don't take me back to the same all-too-familiar recesses where my inner plight and darkness lurked. I chose to step into the light, where I could embrace the shadow of my past self but not let it deter me from living my life to my fullest potential in the present. It became a matter of perspective.

My father and I cried and hugged each other in the orchid garden in Auroville. Papa was back in my life and, as a 28-year-old desperate to be freed from my history, I began to imagine the possibility of being in the world simply as his daughter, his little girl again. I felt light and free from the weight I had been carrying for so many years. Another big layer had just been shed. I could breathe in new life now. At 28, I still had enough innocence to believe that.

Bit by bit I was concluding the previous chapter of my life and releasing all the anger, resentment, and unfinished business I had had with people. I wrote letters to my ex-husband and to his mother, forgiving and asking for forgiveness. I shared extensively with Prema and worked to go deeper in my meditations and healing, to be open, compassionate, and loving regardless of what had happened in my life. I continued my training with her and two of her close colleagues—one from Switzerland, Margaret, and another from Mumbai, Prasad. Together the three of them would launch an organization for transformation called Anahatha, which is the Indian name given to the heart chakra or heart energy center.

In the following months, I trained with the three of them extensively—assisting as well as helping lead smaller group sessions at their retreats and workshops. As an assistant to such powerful transformational leaders, I gained a new perspective on who I was in the world and how I "showed up" for others. Assisting at the seminars was instrumental in fostering my developing awareness and ability to be present to what was going on within me and around me.

As assistants, we were counted on to help with all areas of the seminar to ensure that it ran smoothly. From waking up the participants, bringing the leaders their tea, setting up the room where the session was to be held, and, as part of our own training, doing the participants' assignments and homework in addition to the extra work the seminar leaders assigned to us, the demands and learning curve were steep. We assistants were the last ones to go to bed and the first to wake up, usually between the hours of 1 and 4 a.m. Despite the intense nature of these retreat weekends, they were the most fun times, packed with self-awareness, breakthroughs, and spiritual insights, and this made it all worth it. Being immersed in the work for 72 hours straight with a laser focus on how I could serve the leaders as well as the participants was an experience of great value to me. Serving and training on the ground like this was an exceptional honor and privilege. I remember being so moved by witnessing the participants' transformations that would occur in front of my eyes.

It seemed like once I had set my mind on my own personal healing and transformation, opportunities just kept knocking at my door. One such opportunity arrived a month before my wedding. It was for a fire-walking seminar. *Could this be a coincidence? Maybe I am supposed to do this?* The fire-walking seminar was less about the physical experience of walking on the hot coals and more of a metaphor for facing and conquering your fears. All it really amounted to was a 12-foot-long walk, around four feet wide probably, on which hot burning coals were laid. There was a basin of water on the other end of the walk that you could step into. I remember I kept letting everyone in front of me and just couldn't get myself to go across. Crying bitterly, I realized that my deepest fear was not having love in my life. In that moment, I remember Prema's voice reassuring me that I could do it. I also remember saying to myself that I was giving up all fears of being in a loving, trusting relationship and getting married. After I had completed the fire-walk, I felt I had ripped open my heart and extracted every last bit of fear, doubt, and worry. I was certain that I had left no stone unturned and shed all that needed shedding. Now I had healed every possible nook and cranny of my mental, emotional, and spiritual self. I was ready to be a bride once again.

Kash, Love, and Marriage

Kash was due to arrive on the 9th of February, just five days before the wedding. Between those five days in February and the 12 days he visited the previous year, Kash and I had spent a total of 17 days together, in person and in the same city, prior to making our vows. We had a beautiful Indian wedding at a place called The Amethyst in Chennai, a venue that had once served as the summer palace of the Maharaja of Jaipur and later became a rundown dump. Now renovated and restored to its old-world charm, it was the perfect setting for our ceremony.

After the honeymoon, Kash returned to the U.S. and I waited in India for the American embassy to issue my visa. And when that finally happened, on June 25, 2002, I flew to Washington Dulles Airport and landed in the U.S.A. for the first time. Kash was there to receive me. He brought me home, carried me over the threshold, and a new chapter in our lives began.

The first few years of our marriage were packed with fun, adventure, and financial challenge. Kash had started an Internet company the year the so-called "bubble" burst in 1999. Strapped with payroll and business expenses, he and his business partners held back their own paychecks, making no money for months on end. I decided to look for a job to help us pay our bills. I walked into a temporary staffing agency after my online application had been accepted. After a brief conversation and a test of my ability to work with Microsoft Word and Excel, I was told I had a job and would start the next day. Very pleased with myself, I walked out the door, not knowing, asking, or even caring how much I was going to be paid or what the nature of the job was. My friends who know me today will completely get that that would be me! I got back in the car where Kash was eager to hear the aforementioned details that I didn't think to investigate. I went back into the office and returned with all the information I didn't think to gather in the first place. I was told that I was going to be paid $15 an hour and would be working for a local home mortgage firm.

A job in the U.S., starting tomorrow, oh, oh! I had no idea what I was supposed to do and how I was going to do it, but something inside me said I would be fine. I knew this would be a challenge, but I always loved being challenged. I wore a red skirt-and-jacket suit on my first day that I borrowed from my mother-in-law. I was later told I was overdressed for my temporary, entry-level position, but it didn't stop me; I always liked being dressed professionally. If I was going to do this, then I was going to do this right and play the part well!

We had phones and mobiles back in India, but I had never needed extensions, or to mute a call, or conference someone in before, so this whole office experience was foreign to me. Although I adequately managed to perform my first duties—collecting hazard insurance documentation by phone—I didn't let anyone know I was outside my comfort zone. I will never forget my first time sending a fax. I had no idea how the fax machine worked. I went into the copy room and pretended I was putting away some papers and watched as another employee was sending faxes. I quietly observed where he loaded the documents, punched in some numbers, and then off it went. "I could do that," I thought to myself. A first successful attempt built my confidence as I became more comfortable in this environment.

My supervisor, Donna, was so impressed with the speed and efficiency with which I was getting my work done that within two weeks she promoted me from the phones to entering data into the computer for the client loan applications. Two weeks after that I was processing loans and beginning to work closely with the loan officers, helping them get their deals closed. I was still making $15 an hour and this work was not hard at all; it was just a new kind of work. At first it was interesting, but the minute it got easy, I wanted more. Less than two months into my job, real estate lingo had become part of my vocabulary. Now I not only knew what hazard insurance was, I also knew what title insurance, deed of trust, real estate taxes, mortgage insurance, FHA, URLA, and HUD meant. After about two months of processing files, I was offered a permanent position and became a full-time employee with all the benefits. Six months into being a full-time loan processor, I requested a promotion to become sales assistant to the loan advisor and switched over from operations to sales. My journey in corporate America was moving really fast. Six months after becoming a sales assistant, I asked to become an independent loan advisor, which I did.

I don't think I paused for a moment to even think about where I was headed and what I was really doing or where I was going. I was simply speeding down the highway of my new American life. Looking back, I was in such survival mode, I just kept doing what I needed to do in order to keep my job, impress my employer, and be a stellar worker bee in order to make an income. I don't remember thinking, even once, what it was that I actually wanted in life beyond being married to the man I loved and building a life together.

With hindsight, it is clear to me now that I had entered the rat race and was competing like everyone else to get more sales, close more loans, and rank high on the spreadsheet at the end of the month when employee performance was measured. My first day at that job was the last day I did my full morning-meditation practice. I just never found the time to "pause" for my usual length of time and reflect after that. I had completely stopped all of my transformational and spiritual work. No hour-long sitting in meditation and chanting mantras every morning. No time to clean my altar, put out fresh flowers, or light incense. Instead, I was unconsciously taking a little side trip to examine where this new chapter of my life would lead me.

Within months of migrating to the United States, I was working for one of the leading banks. It was all happening so fast. My meditations were now parceled into three- or four- or five-minute segments throughout the day, and I did a drive-by salute to my Buddhas on the altar as I left in the mornings. I would take a few minutes while riding the metro or while on the bus to close my eyes and take a few energizing deep breaths. I used my lunch break to eat quietly by myself, not to be antisocial but to get the 15 minutes to just step away from it all and assimilate my thoughts, and pause—more briefly than I had in the past but with meditative focus nonetheless. Every now and again I would place my hands on my abdomen or knees and spend five or ten minutes doing Reiki on myself. Just those few snatches of deep breathing, pausing, and stepping out of the "busy-ness" would help revive and rejuvenate me. My colleagues wondered how I had so much energy and was never exhausted at 5 p.m. I didn't even realize what I was doing; I definitely didn't appreciate it consciously. It was more subtle. I didn't have the time to slow down and check in with myself and see what actions in my life were working and which ones weren't. And so, although I felt guilty for going away from my formal practice, I had failed to notice that these mini-pauses I created worked as a way to recharge myself. The self-awareness practices I had integrated into my life prior to moving to the U.S. had become my new default setting. I just couldn't acknowledge it at the time; ironically I was unaware that I was aware. There was a divine intelligence that was sourcing the fuel it needed to keep the life force flowing through me, helping me prosper in my life.

I was now a busy executive, with one hand on the steering wheel and the other perpetually on my Blackberry. Standard business hours did not apply; I was available 24/7. During the week I was working with my team to close loans and get the loans through the underwriting process, consulting with clients, and taking new loan applications. On the weekends I was helping real estate agents with open houses, writing up pre-approval letters and following up with new leads. I was completely transformed into someone I couldn't recognize anymore. There was no healing practice or work as an actress. No auditions anymore, photo shoots, hair and make-up sessions. I was living in a whole new world where there were no transformational seminars or Reiki classes. Even though I had spent 18 months with the massage community at the Potomac Massage Training Institute, my connection to the holistic practices were becoming a distant memory. I never discussed that part of my life with anyone—I was now working in the mortgage business.

Like a chameleon, I had once again adapted my personality based on where I was and the role I needed to play in order to survive in my new environment. People commented that the American lifestyle suited me. Few believed I had been in the country only a couple of years and was already so successful. It was like I was born to be American, truly. I felt at home and never pursued the potential of acting or energy work in the Washington, DC, area. I just assumed it was pointless and offered no future. Now I had a "real" job and had to work like "real" people worked. I was not an entitled little princess-actress with an entourage.

I didn't have a driver's license for several months after coming to the U.S., and Kash had to drive me a distance of 30 miles across a state line, on major highways and in rush-hour traffic, every morning. After work in the evenings, I would walk to a bus stop and catch a train to a station closer to home where he would pick me up.

During my first winter in America, I hadn't learned yet how to dress in layers. I didn't have the weather-appropriate clothes and shoes. I had one tan winter coat I used for everything, and due to limited funds bought shoes that cost no more than $20. My feet hurt so badly by the evening, I would get home crying. But I would always wipe my tears away before Kash saw me. I couldn't let him see me hurting or in pain. I never complained, never wanting to be a problem or a burden. I wanted to only be helpful and support Kash and this new life with my head held up high. I just told myself I needed to toughen up and be strong, never once suspecting that all I needed was just better shoes. It seems strange from my perspective now, but we were very stressed economically at the time and I also suspect now that my pattern of sucking up discomfort or unease was one I acquired at a young age in learning to keep things to myself, silencing myself and hiding the pain.

In all this time I never shared anything about my past with Kash. At the age of 17, Kash had lost his father to alcohol abuse that led to suicide, and now he got along really well with my dad. I felt it would be selfish of me to compromise my father's image in Kash's eyes since he was the next best thing my husband had to a father. I didn't want to disappoint him and rob him of that relationship. In so doing, I was choosing what was best for Kash without giving him the chance to choose freely. I figured that I had already dealt with all that history. I was convinced there would never be any need for Kash to know because I believed that my relationship with my father was completely healed. *Why bring that energy into my new life? That was then, this is now. He doesn't need to know. What for?*

Unconsciously, I was repeating the exact behavior that my mother had requested of me with respect to my brothers' relationships with my father. *I'll stay silent so at least Kash can have a clean and pure relationship with my dad.* There was still this need to protect my dad—and perhaps me and Kash as well. *Wouldn't my telling Kash end my fairy-tale marriage?* I couldn't let that happen.

And then I became a mother.

Babies

When Kash and I found out we were pregnant with our first baby, we were very excited. I knew in my heart that it was going to be a boy. We didn't find out the sex of the baby prior to the birth because we wanted it to be a surprise. Well, a surprise it was. Ananya was a baby girl, a beautiful little ball of love. We had brought blue clothes and blankies to the hospital. *Well, never mind,* I thought. *The next one would be a boy.*

Rena, our second beautiful baby girl, was born on February 2, 2006. She was cute as a button and of course we just adored her. But I looked up, my eyes peering into the skies above, asking the Universe for the punch line to this cosmic joke, because I wasn't laughing. I thought God and I had a deal, that not having to worry about being a mother to daughters was in the contract. *Go through all that again? No, thank you.* I trusted Kash completely, of course, but I had a sense that being a mother to girls would remind me of my past, and so I would have to be very vigilant on their behalf to protect them. Above all, I couldn't allow myself to be the failure I felt my mother to be, and in this respect, having daughters who could potentially be subjected to abuse from someone was an added burden for me. There was no denying that I loved, absolutely loved, becoming a mother to my darling daughters, and deep within me, below the negotiations with my grief and a higher power, I knew, ultimately, especially after the birth of my third daughter, that they had come to heal me.

Can you protect me from yourself? These words, which the character Frodo spoke in *The Lord of the Rings*, a movie trilogy that I loved, resonated with me in my relationship with my daughters. I didn't want my daughters to have to be shielded from me and my past. I, the protective lioness of a mother, with all my best intentions, love, and encouragement—how could I own my journey and allow them theirs? One of my all-time favorite poets Kahlil Gibran wrote:

> *Your children are not your children.*
> *They are the sons and daughters of life's longing for itself.*
> *They come through you but not from you.*
> *And though they are with you yet they belong not to you.*
> *You may give them your love but not your thoughts. For*
> *they have their own thoughts.*
> *You may house their bodies but not their souls. For their*
> *souls dwell in the house of tomorrow, which you can-*
> *not visit, not even in your dreams.*
> *You may strive to be like them, but seek not to make them*
> *like you. For life goes not backward nor tarries with*
> *yesterday.*

These words have been the source of much hope and healing for me. When I read this, I can feel a gentle breeze flow through me—one that reminds me that all is well in my world. My daughters are well. This is exactly where we are supposed to be.

On May 8, 2009, we were blessed with our third daughter, Aishwarya. By then I knew that this was more a cosmic plan than a cosmic joke. Instead of battling the winds, I embraced them and let them move me in the direction of my destiny. My three little goddesses have unknowingly helped me, one step at a time, to get clearer and closer to living my life's purpose—to live my life as authentically as possible, to be self-expressed and to allow the message of healing and transformation to be shared in the world.

Opening Up to Kash

Even though I did not have a full-time transformation practice during the early months of being in America, there was always something slowly but surely drawing me back to the work of meditation and healing. In my first year after moving, I had enrolled myself into the massage therapy program at the Potomac Massage Training Institute (PMTI) in Washington, DC. I had no idea how this training would eventually play out in my life as I was by then a successful mortgage advisor. But it was nourishing to feel connected to a tribe of individuals with whom I felt very comfortable, to whom I could relate, and with whom I could engage in conversations around transformation and healing touch. Twice a week the classes in DC helped me step away from the intense finance industry and step back into the awareness of the body, mind, and spirit connection.

I believe that those 18 months at PMTI provided much. Eventually, when it came time to leave the mortgage business, massage was the segue that brought me back to the healing that comes with transformation practices, which eventually became a full-time occupation and life purpose. Although it superficially looks like someone massaging another is only manipulating the body's soft tissue, in reality it impacted all of me by helping me get present, even if it was to muscles, aches, and pains, or even to which oils to use. It delivered the pause I needed to reflect on who I had transformed into since I had arrived in the United States after being married, having three children, a new house, and a career in mortgages that I had never expected. Having national board certifications and licensing as a massage therapist would help me immediately find a job at a national massage therapy chain while simultaneously starting my own practice from home.

I remember being at a community event and talking with a chiropractor about what I did. In a few weeks, I got a call from him asking how he could have "personal transformation" in his life. One by one people called to set up a time to meet so they could transform and heal their lives. Slowly, massage clients started to turn into transformation clients. Those clients then wondered what was next for them after a series of one-on-one sessions. The Anahatha–I AM Retreats were born from this in order to give people the opportunity to experience transformation at the group level. The retreats ran from Friday through Sunday. The participants would come to claim a safe and sacred space for themselves, to pause, reflect, renew, and rejuvenate. They would leave having shed years and years of pain, anger, and unnecessary baggage. Above all, at this technology-free weekend, they would be guided in a variety of meditations and transformative practices and yoga.

About a week or two after returning from leading an I AM Love and Aliveness in Relationships Retreat and during one of my meditations, I had a vision of Kash and me sitting on a bench watching the ocean waves come crashing in onto the beach. We just sat there in silence, witnesses to the beauty in front of us as well as the calm within us. In this vision we are both old, probably in our 80s. In that moment, my elderly self wondered how our life could have been different if I had had complete emotional, physical, and spiritual intimacy with this man I had been married to for over 50 years. How would "this" moment have been different if I had been able to be healed and liberated from carrying my secret in our relationship?

When I came out of my meditation, I knew with profound clarity that I did not want to live to regret not having lived my life 100 percent. Was it going to be easy? No, but not living in integrity with this vision was not an option. What's the worst that could happen? I could tell Kash and he would feel betrayed that I kept this from him and he might want to leave me. Or he will learn why I have been trying to be the father *and* the mother to the girls, do it all, be it all, fight to be heard and seen. He might embrace me with love and compassion. Either way, we would both know the truth.

I remember the exact day I told him and couldn't hold back my tears as I shared with him from my heart. I explained why my reactions and responses to certain things were the way they were. Why I didn't like watching *CSI SVU* (*Special Victims Unit*), a television show that mainly solves crimes related to rape and sexual assault; why I had an issue with giving permission for sleepovers for the girls; why I sometimes would be irritable in discussions surrounding my father. Kash, equally emotional, hugged me and said he was so sorry that I had gone through the pain and anguish of this experience as well as having kept this secret. He was not mad at my father because as the person he knows my father to be today, he can see how hard he has worked to turn his life around.

I saw how I had to step into the very work of Love and Aliveness in Relationships Retreat that I had taught a fortnight ago. Just teaching the work to my students and clients wasn't enough. Living my life in integrity meant a commitment to always challenge the status quo, forever giving me the opportunity to elevate my inner awareness, deepen my understanding of myself, and help me move in the direction of my life's fullest expression, vision, and purpose. It was never clearer to me than the day I unveiled my true self to my husband and surrendered. In that moment, I was not only surrendering to the trust I had in our love, but also trusting that I was safe in sharing my truths with him, that our lives were meant to be joined, and that this was a step in the right direction. I also realized that this idea that life should one day become all rainbows and puppies absent any conflict was not real. Sometimes life was just a mush of all unprocessed feelings, messy and off kilter. I didn't have to lose my mind over it. Just notice it, be with it, and let it be with me. It was OK that my life was not going to be OK all the time.

The more I taught, the more I learned. Every student, client, and participant who came into my life was there for a reason. In the seven years since 2008 that I have been working with clients individually, in retreats, and in workshops, I continue to peel back the layers of my own life, seeing my vulnerability with greater clarity and recognizing my strengths as well as opportunities for growth.

Throughout my life, the Universe has been whispering messages into my ear and I was finally starting to pay attention. The Cosmic Plan had trumped Plans A, B, and C, and I was finally beginning to integrate my multiple personas while shedding false identities. For the first time I felt what it was like to relate to my partner in complete transparency and emotional intimacy. I felt so liberated and free—such a big weight was lifted off my shoulders and I realized what a burden I had been carrying for such a long time. I no longer needed to wait for permission to speak my truth. I was able to speak the unspeakable. My longing to live fully self-expressed was met by my calling to help others heal and transform. And as a mother to three growing girls, I have the honor to witness and guide their journey in this life. I am a wife to an amazing man whom I met when I was four and he was three, and something tells me we might have met in other lifetimes as well. Above all, I am walking proof that the potential for healing, unconditional love, and forgiveness is right here within us, infinite and ever expanding.

Sexual Healing

At one of the retreats, I led a meditation that involved movement called No Dimensions. It was created by an Indian spiritual teacher and mystic, Osho. In this meditation, the entire group moves in unison with six basic moves and then repeats them over and over again for almost 45 minutes. I was leading this meditation and was in the front row of the group closest to the wall in a cabin we had been in so many times, and I had led this very meditation in the same spot previously. But I had never before noticed a certain piece of bark from a tree nailed onto the wall directly in front of me. On this occasion, however, about 15 minutes into the meditation, I did. From my perspective, the piece of wood looked like a wrinkly, rotten vagina. In my head I heard, *that's my vagina.* That's what I thought it must look like after all of the years of abuse and shame and hiding.

I couldn't stop smiling and giggling to myself for the next 30 minutes. My team thought I was just really happy with the way the meditation was going, the opening of the heart chakra, the energy center for love at the center of our chest, and the commitment of the participants to keep up with the movement. That was all true. But secretly I felt liberated. This was my eighth retreat and the first retreat that Kash had attended.

The image of that piece of bark had given me an opportunity, a mirror to see how I viewed my own sexual self. My old denial and self-limiting beliefs about my body had me believe that I had a rotten, wrinkly, hardened vagina. *Who would want to be intimate with someone whose vagina looked like that?* The realization happened in an instant, and I saw the old programming and realized that this was a false and no longer relevant identity I was carrying. I felt a freedom unlike any other. As the awareness dawned on me, the giggle erupted, loosening this antiquated and limiting self-perception; suddenly I had no reason to hold on to the old story anymore.

I believe that we are always met where we are; in other words, we must fully accept—i.e., be honest about what we think and feel—exactly what is going on in our heads. That is where you are at a given moment, and the very process of accepting with honesty your thoughts and feelings is meeting yourself. Judging or measuring how you are at some other point is not relevant to where you are *right now*. The day I was met by this insight changed my relationship with myself, the way I celebrated my body, and the way I saw myself. I was given the opportunity to truly enjoy my sexuality for the first time, and this was after having been married 10 years to the man I love and giving birth to three wonderful daughters. I learned that it is never too late to love myself and reach new depths of authenticity and renewal.

At the retreats, we provide red, heart-shaped cards to the participants to write out notes and stick them anywhere they want in the cabin. I took a card and wrote *I love my vagina* and stuck it next to this piece of bark nailed to the cabin wall. It did create a new segment—or what I like to call an opportunity for a discussion—at the retreat, one that had never presented itself before.

Just by sharing my own truth and speaking what had previously been unspeakable in my life allowed participants to open up in kind and share their lives with the rest of the group. An implicit faith and trust was born among the retreat participants. People discussed their past abuse and the traumas that they had kept secret for many years, secrets that some had been living with for over 40 years, too afraid to utter the truth. As a result, they too had been held back in several areas of their life, including, in some cases, their sexual ones.

I forget sometimes to pause and acknowledge the challenges, time commitment, and resilience it takes to be grounded. The fun part is that once you start to become aware, you can't go back. I guess one can try, but it's really difficult to become *less* awakened. One insight clears the way to a new level of understanding, and that space tills fertile ground for new insights to grow. For example, while writing this chapter around sexual healing and my breakthrough "vagina" moment at the retreat, I was naked. I did not start out naked; it just happened. It was a warm day, and the doors of the cabin where I had been writing were open for fresh air. There was a beautiful breeze blowing through the room, and I had my hair down. As the sun came up and started shining down through the skylights, it got warmer, and I started taking layers of clothing off as I was writing. I realized toward the end of the chapter how this had happened only for this chapter and no other. Talk about "embodying" the work. I was laughing by myself in the cabin at the end of the chapter, chuckling as I noticed how far I had come—from believing that I was that wrinkly piece of bark to feeling secure and light with my naked self.

Like most healing, sexual healing cannot be rushed or forced. But with space, time, and awareness, it can happen. In fact, it will happen, if you allow it.

For as long as I believed something to be true, I always found evidence to prove this belief right, like a self-fulfilling prophecy. If I felt I was not good enough, I found evidence of that in how people looked at me, what they said to me, and how they said it. I still see people with this sort of "persecution complex" and sadly I understand it all too well. Fortunately, the transformation and meditation practices have helped in retraining my mind and quieting its incessant chatter.

Forgiveness

Forgiveness is necessary but can be tricky. I have seen some spiritual teachers ask that you drop all negative emotions, have a release, forgive others, forgive yourself, and move on. That's it. But I don't believe forgiveness can be totally summoned that way. In my experience, forgiveness, like transformation, has layers and phases. One cannot just flip a switch. At least, it did not work like that for me. But once I became aware and fully present to my circumstances, then paused to forgive meaningfully with intention and clarity, my life changed forever.

There is a period of time during the healing process when forgiveness is not even an option, and people who suggest otherwise are damn insensitive fools, as I like to call them. Forgiveness cannot be forced. Like everything else in life, you are ready when you are ready. It is important to fully feel where you are along the way and the attendant emotions—the anger, blame, and shame. Truly being with the process as it unfolds, however it unfolds, is being true to your journey. Each step along the way is a valid place to be, and since you cannot be any place other than where you are, you may as well embrace it. The trick is to know it is OK *not* to be OK.

On the other hand, it is instructive to notice to what end, and for how long, you are withholding forgiveness. How do you experience this life while still holding on to resentment and anger? How are your relationships being impacted by not forgiving? Not forgiving is a choice we make, and like any choice, it has consequences. Are we willing to accept the consequences of not forgiving in our life? If you hope to flourish with love, laughter, and freedom in your life, how does holding on to an unforgiven past impact that? If you want to be in a relationship one day where you can be 100 percent present to your partner, how does not forgiving an ex or a parent impact that possibility for your future? Are you withholding forgiveness because you still want the person who inflicted the pain to suffer equally, if not more? If so, who is really suffering? Is holding back forgiveness inadvertently your strategy for revenge?

I can understand that if it is.

Eventually, we get so used to coexisting with our not-so-good feelings that to be without them is a greater pain to bear. Relinquishing this cocoon of familiarity requires a realignment and reorganization of our habitual thought processes. It is my belief and experience that denying and delaying forgiveness only holds you back. It is disadvantageous to progress and a debilitating hindrance to growth and happiness, at best. The dilemma is that those yucky feelings actually make us feel safe, because we have been around them for so long. To dismiss them now is like cutting off one's own limb. Unfortunately, there is a cost associated with *not* letting go of those not-so-good, albeit familiar, feelings. Without intentionally tapping into your pain and potential for forgiveness, "moving on" is a Band-Aid and a cover up for the hurting self. We live by denying ourselves access to peace and happiness.

When a wound is not treated in time, it gets infected. If infection festers, it may start to spread and systemically affect other areas of the body. To heal the wound after it has become systemic, you have to approach the entire body and not just that one part where the wound originated. The process of forgiveness as a tool for transformation works a little bit like healing that systemic wound. It is critical for reclaiming your wholeness, but it doesn't have to be rushed. It's there for us when we are ready, and we just have to make sure we are checking in occasionally.

I have seen support groups for survivors of abuse and watched online forums as well to see how participants interact with each other. Decades after the abuse, there is still unprocessed anger and shame. There is still the "me against the abuser" rhetoric. I find that such groups of people gravitate toward one another. We love what is familiar even if it is painful, usually because even those things that cause pain may seem safer than the unknown. The repeated use of the terms "victim" and "survivor" continue to foster feelings of powerlessness, giving one another permission to stay in a perpetual state of opposition and blame. Reading the conversations on online forums and social media pages has actually left me feeling quite depressed, angry, and anxious about my own life.

There was a time when I too defined myself as a victim and then a survivor of sexual abuse. But then one day it hit me that I was not another label or tag. I was neither victim nor survivor; I was just a girl who had a series of experiences that led me on a journey. I am still on that journey and don't feel I need to give myself any more labels. So I choose not to use the words "victim" or "survivor" anymore although I do not dismiss or underestimate the experiences, repercussions, or imprints of my past. Yes, that happened, and it was terrible, but it was a long time ago. But let us not continue to define ourselves based on what happened in the past and thus put ourselves in a box. Let us shed the identity of the old self. I want for us all to liberate ourselves from labeling ourselves. To someone else we may be our social security number, our race, our gender, our socioeconomic status, our title, our sexual orientation, our political agenda, and so forth. This disintegration of self does not serve us. Let us not divide ourselves up anymore and instead think of ourselves as the embodiment of love—love for ourselves, love for others. I can thrive with that self-label; all others, such as "warrior" or "survivor," are one-dimensional and therefore false.

My request to all the men and women in the support groups is to try to get what is true for you into your conscious mind. It is comforting to be part of a tribe that "gets" you and understands where you have been and how it must feel to have suffered the way you did. This is an important place to hang out for a while, but it is only one stop on the journey. After a while, I invite you to try to move toward the possibility of forgiveness, love, and compassion. The reason you may not have ventured totally and completely in that direction is that you felt it was safer for you not to. I know the feeling. I felt that way too for a very long time. But I also know that it is possible to move beyond this feeling. If it happened for me, it can happen for you. It can happen for anyone.

Motherhood

Having daughters has helped me heal myself. Watching them grow into young ladies and looking forward to their continued maturation into adults give me vicarious opportunities to understand how I might have taken on the beliefs I did when I did. Being a mother to my three girls is a

gift that helps me face my own fears and teach them to feel empowered
by the love they have for themselves, unpolluted by fear. I want them to
have wholesome opportunities to learn about their bodies, to learn about
safe and unsafe touch, and to always celebrate being women.

But as much as I continue to be present and work on healing myself,
every now and again I find myself being challenged as a mother in certain situations.

I was about to attend a Rosen Method Bodywork Intensive in Berke-
ley, CA, about the time the 2008 opening ceremonies of the Beijing Olym-
pics had begun. As I was heading to the airport to go to this therapeutic
bodywork seminar, something that had been hibernating within me woke
up. Some "what if" scenarios regarding my father loomed in my mind,
bringing up all kinds of worrisome thoughts about my growing daughters. *Would they be safe around him? Will I ever be able to let them just
go visit their grandparents on their own? What if my mother dies before
my father? How will we deal with that situation if that happens?* My
mind just kept going on and on in what I consider a classic case of trying
to suppress the shadow self—the part of my subconscious mind where
my darkest, most negative thoughts lay hiding.

This deeper layer came to awareness several years after the healing session in the orchid garden with my father. I called my father from the
Rosen Intensive bawling my guts out. I was afraid—so terrified of the
unknown—and I shared that with him. I asked him how could I be certain that he wouldn't make advances toward my girls. I still hadn't spoken
to Kash or any of my close friends about my past, so no one knew what I
was battling on the inside. When I'd say that my parents were visiting
from India, people would naturally think that it was a good thing or that
it would be so nice for the kids to visit with their grandparents. No one
knew what an excruciating thought that was for me; to have my father
around my girls, risking their safety, and to have my mother around, not
knowing if she would even know there was something amiss if something
happened and if she would be completely be out of touch with reality,
like she had been with me when I was little. When I spoke to him over the
phone, crying, I know I let my fear and vulnerability show. There was no
point in hiding it. Yes, we had done a lot of therapeutic work together, we
had healed, forgiven, and transformed. But now there was a new context—a context that involved my daughters. This was a new layer, a new
level. This could not have been confronted before because it didn't exist

until now. If my father and I were to have any chance at a continued relationship in the coming years, then we had to connect authentically to be in each other's lives—we needed to establish boundaries.

I remember feeling like he thought my fears were ridiculous and that my having them or being gripped by this terror in this way was just nonsense. In other words, I don't think he took me seriously. I thought to myself that perhaps I was going overboard too, undermining my own authenticity.

On another occasion, when my oldest was seven years old, she had been making requests for sleepovers at her friends' homes. I remember so many undesirable thoughts flashed through my mind within an instant. *What if? What if? What if?* I recalled that as a child myself, the idea of going over to a friend's place for a sleepover was fun and exciting. But now, as a mother, the idea of my girls doing so seemed scary and an absolute NO-NO! While the arguments—pros, cons—and opinions regarding this thought are limitless, my little girl always negotiated and seldom took no for an answer.

Once I had told Kash all about my history, I remember openly discussing this particular dilemma with him and he said that he understood how I felt but that I shouldn't project my fears and hold my girls back from living their lives. It was just what I needed to hear, because that was what I *wanted* too. I didn't want my daughters to have to be protected from me like Frodo in *The Lord of the Rings*.

The kinds of insights that came with being a mother have helped me grow beyond my imagination. They have given me the opportunity to recognize whether I am making choices for my children that are based in fear or based in love. And when I discover I am making a choice based in fear, I choose to reframe how I am seeing things in the present moment. It's a conscious choice that I can make. I don't have to be stuck in my past. I now find myself having the permission to relax, let go, and allow my girls their journey. My fears were not only keeping me from being present to the opportunities for fun and laughter in our lives, above all they were limiting my girls, my reason to be and to exist. It just didn't make sense to want freedom and then live in a cage for the rest of our lives.

I welcome these opportunities to grow and expand my consciousness in my life. I am grateful for these moments of awareness of myself so I can get unstuck and heal some more. Because when I get unstuck and heal, transformation happens. And that empowers me.

I acknowledge this transition happening within me and have made love-based choices on the subject of sleepovers. My girls have spent a weekend on two occasions now with friends whom our family is very close to. It took my getting fully present and reaffirming that transformation is not a destination, it is a journey.

I don't think I could have been as present as I am today as a mother, a wife, and a mentor if not for the work I have done on forgiveness. Practicing forgiveness meant that I had to let go of blaming my father, pointing the finger and handing over all responsibility for my happiness to others. Right now, I can say that I am blossoming emotionally, mentally, and spiritually.

Gratitude

When I realized that I love the person I have become despite what has happened in my life, I feel so much gratitude for where this journey has led me. But if I feel gratitude for the present moment, how can I not also feel gratitude for the moments that went before? How can I not have gratitude for my past experiences, good, bad, or indifferent? How can I have complete gratitude for my husband, my children, my participants, and my students and not have gratitude for my father, my mother, my teachers, and my ex-partners? I would not be here today, writing this memoir, helping and guiding others on their journey of forgiveness and healing, if it had not been for my past experiences and exposures.

If I am to acknowledge the present as a blessing in my life, which I do, then the same is true for everything that brought me to this moment.

Commentary

What is in the highest good of the whole is in the highest good for each one of us. As is the microcosm, so is the macrocosm. Saying that your fate is not tied to mine is like saying your end of the boat is sinking. What's interesting is also how the mind justifies our fears for us. The story I made up was that because I was the recipient of childhood abuse and molestation, my children are not safe and under no circumstance will I ever, ever let them out of my sight. What a gift to all of us to be able to shift our fear-based choices to love-based choices.

Questions for Self-Introspection

●	Do you find yourself occasionally making fear-based choices?
●	Is there a pattern or story around an area of your life that causes you to be stuck in making fear-based choices?
●	If you knew that you could release the old pattern of making those fear-based choices, would you be willing to experience transformation?
●	What would your life look like if moving forward you made choices based in love?
●	Write out a scenario in your life where you would make choices based on love and not fear.

5

Tools for Transformation

O ccasionally I am asked if I teach a specific technique. That is a valid question but my answer isn't simple, or short. Over the years I have studied both Eastern and Western philosophies from teachers all over the world. While I spent the initial part of my life in India and was influenced by teachers there, my appetite for learning all I possibly could on the subject of healing, metaphysics, energy, and personal development expanded well beyond the country of India. Some of my teachers and influences other than Prema include Louise Hay, Osho, J. Krishnamurti, Dr. Deepak Chopra, Dr. Paula Horan, and Marion Rosen.

In addition, throughout my childhood I attended different schools that taught various disciplines—among them philosophical, Catholic, and Hindu—that broadened my spiritual perspective.

I was always drawn to nonfiction books more than fiction, and our home library was stocked with volumes such as *Jonathan Livingston Seagull, Zen and the Art of Motorcycle Maintenance*, and the *I Ching*. I remember reading Richard Bach and J. Krishnamurti well before I understood the abstract existential concepts and philosophies they wrote about.

As I grew older, I bought books with my own saved-up pocket money such as the *Chicken Soup* series by Jack Canfield and *Conversations with God* by Neale Donald Walsch. During the '80s and '90s, reading these books one by one, I absorbed and assimilated the teachings that would one day help my own healing philosophy evolve out of some of the profound insights I gleaned from their work that resonated with me.

Of all the body work and transformation techniques I studied, I believe it was Reiki that helped me the most initially. It might have been the meditative quality combined with the light touch that synthesized body, mind, and spirit. These hands-on healing sessions were always deeply relaxing and rejuvenating.

I have also studied with some of the best teachers there are in modalities such as feng shui, Bach flowers, massage therapy, Ayurveda, yoga, chanting, and the Rosen method of bodywork. I have personally experienced the benefits of these therapeutic modalities as well as worked closely with an incredible group of masters and mentors. All these healing approaches have helped me get in touch with my own truth and voice. This enabled me to develop my own inner awareness, instinct, and intuition as a teacher, formulate my own message, and present it to the world as "I AM—Inner Awareness Manifestation," or what I call the "I AM Consciousness."

I don't see myself as a teacher of a specific sect, style, or form of meditation, transformation, spirituality, or belief system. I would rather not create distinctions that separate one lineage or style from another. I see my body of work as all encompassing, inclusive, and primarily a self-expression of my experiences on the spiritual journey of my life. I feel fortunate to have had an awakening at the right moment in time to join the dance of the cosmos. I continue to pause in silent witness to this awareness within me and my search for a deeper understanding of human existence.

> The effects of motivation fade away. So do the effects of bathing, which is why we recommend it every day.
> —Zig Ziglar

When my healing began during a retreat, the insights and experience were deeply profound. But when the retreat came to an end and everyone had to go home, I found myself wanting the work to continue. What was I supposed to do? Besides, we all have existential questions in our lives, questions like *Why?* or *Why me?* or *Why did so and so do this to me?* or *What am I supposed to do?* or *Where am I supposed go from here?*

This quandary led me to an insight that I paraphrase and display on a poster at my retreats:

If you ask a question, expect the answer.

Participants often ignore it at first: "What's the big deal in that?"

In short, the big deal is that if you can learn to listen, your inner voice will answer you.

When we ask those existential questions like *Why me?*, every so often our inner voice may at first respond with answers such as, *I don't know. Maybe because you suck and this is your destiny, you're not worthy, you're not good enough, you are rotten, you are damaged*, and on and on.

I reached a point, as does anyone exposed to other possibilities, where I began to question the validity of that voice. I know it seems like it's "the" voice, but it's not. If we've been steeped in negative and damaging relationships, chances are that the voice we hear may be tainted by these influences. Your true inner voice would speak to you with love and compassion. It would speak to you the way you would speak to your friend or your beloved whom you cared for more than anything or anyone in the world.

Shouldn't we give ourselves enough time to allow the cacophony of the negative, self-limiting thoughts from that inner voice run their course until they fatigue and fade away? And in the stillness that follows, shouldn't we leave time to allow the grace and beauty of our true inner light shine through and reach us?

What happens when you run water through a faucet that hasn't been opened for years? What does the water look like at first? It's nasty and disgusting, and we know to let it run until it is clear. Our thoughts charge at us with nothing but the old negating self, and we don't let the water run long enough to reach the springs of the divine spirit within us.

The essence of *If you ask a question, expect the answer* lies in becoming present and surrendering to the moment. It lies in having the mindset of the spiritual seeker willing to bathe in the ubiquitous cascades of divine light. Every answer you need is already within you. You just have to get quiet so that you can listen. You need to have the attitude that the answer may not be apparent at the start, but trust that it will come.

I AM Consciousness

In a deep state of inner reflection in a meditation, the letters I, A, and M kept hovering in my mind's eye. I asked, *What does this mean? What is*

I AM? Why are you showing these letters to me like this? As I stated earlier in this chapter, the message I received is that I AM is Inner Awareness Manifestation. In order to live your life powerfully, you must first know who you are and why you are who you are, become aligned with your inner divine self, and then be the cosmic being you were always meant to be. That is your I AM Consciousness.

And just like that, the I AM Consciousness program was born. Slowly, more messages came in my meditations and visions. They were clear, holographic renditions of the meditation, step by step by step. There would be three phases of the I AM Consciousness program, and the messages I was receiving literally gave me the structure, format, and the content of the course. I have no other way of explaining this. It has probably been the most spiritually significant and creative period of my life in this work. There would be a total of 21 sessions, spread over the course of 11 months—one session every other week.

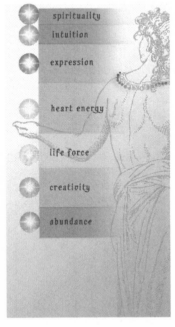

Phase 1—Meeting your inner self: The first phase is to connect with your inner self—see who you are, why you are who you are, what your world looks like, and how you feel about it. In this awakening stage, you begin to see the layers of your past belief systems and self-negating patterns and start to shed and release them one by one, one energy center or chakra at a time. (A chakra is a vortex of energy along the midline of your body. There are seven main chakras that begin from above the top of your head to the base of your spine.) This phase lasted around 11 sessions.

Phase 2—Becoming aligned with your divine self: In the second phase of I AM Consciousness, you become aware that within you is a divine self. You see yourself without the layers of the past and focus on the life you truly desire. Once you see who you truly are meant to be, using guided meditations and visualization techniques you begin to align your vibration to match the vibration of your manifesting divine self. This phase, one of the most creative phases of the program, takes around six sessions.

Phase 3—Connecting with your cosmic self: In the final phase, having shed the past and seen your true divine self, you are now ready to connect with your cosmic self. Your cosmic self is your higher consciousness, your God self—knowing that you are stardust, "no less than the trees and the stars" (see Max Ehrmann, *Desiderata*, on page 101). You see clearly now that you have always been cosmic perfection; all you had to do was reconnect with it. In this phase, you receive several tools and techniques that will help support you in creating an empowered spiritual practice. The phase is around four sessions long, with the last session being graduation.

During the 11-month journey in the I AM Consciousness program, you meet yourself again but in a new paradigm, without the stories, burdens, and layers of the past. As you see your true self emerging, you'll discover that you've always been there, right beneath the layers. You always have. You just needed to find yourself again.

My personal meditation practice helped reveal the structure of the classes, the 11-month program, and the 40 meditations. It all kept pouring into and out of me; little by little, the I AM Consciousness meditation blossomed into a 21-session program for personal transformation and spiritual growth. What started out on a paper napkin in a restaurant when a client was a no-show turned into my most successful course.

Where to Start?

Below I list various tools that I bring to transformation work; in addition, you may find further information on my website at www.Richa Badami.com, which explains more about my programs, and how to get started.

Free audio, video, and text content:

1. My newsletter

2. Richa Badami TV, my YouTube Channel, where I post my video blogs under the series called *Pause for Power*

3. "Something to Pause About," my podcast on iTunes where I post meditations, talks, and interviews

Live events online and in person:

1. I speak regularly at educational events and conferences

2. I lead guided meditations via web stream online

Courses:

1. 11 Secrets to an Empowered Life—video series excerpted from The Guidelines listed at the end of this chapter

2. I AM Consciousness Program—11-month course for spiritual growth and personal transformation

Retreats:

1. I AM Consciousness

2. I AM Love and Aliveness

3. I AM Self-Expression

4. I AM Inner Power

5. I AM Abundance and Prosperity

Graduate and team training:

1. Graduate retreats

2. I AM Anahatha team training

I AM Retreats

How do you pack to pursue a dream and what do you leave behind?

—Sandra Sharpe

When I launched the first I AM Retreat in the United States, I required that participants surrender their cell phones, iPads, laptops, or any other form of digital distractions. These are the current equivalent of the novels that I had carried with me to avoid what was going on with me. If BlackBerrys or iPhones had existed in 1997, I can see myself never looking up at anyone, just staying engrossed in what is now Facebook, Twitter, and, of course, email.

When the "retreaters" first find out that this is a requirement, a few choose not to come. To stay away from their phone for 48 hours is apparently too much to ask. They are just not ready to start the work. But most attendees are now so accustomed to this "Be in the here and now" guideline discussed at the end of this chapter that they preempt us and just start turning in their phones before we even ask them.

In my first retreat while discussing the guideline, I was faced with some resistance, so it took a few minutes to explain its significance. Forty-eight hours later, that same group said their good-byes, hugged each other, picked up their bags, and walked out of the cabin. Not one single participant remembered to ask for the phone back. I have this on tape!

As they were leaving, I called out to them. "Aren't you forgetting something?" Their reaction was a matter-of-fact one.

"Oh, right, yes, the phone. I am not turning that thing on until Monday morning."

Success.

It's not until after experiencing the retreat that the participants fully get the purpose of the guidelines herein. The work that happens in the retreat is so interactive and dynamic that it takes being in the group energy, experiencing the meditations over three days, to fully get the sense. Some retreat participants have given extraordinary testimonials that have affirmed that this is working for them.

Don't get me wrong; this work isn't a fit for everyone. As Pema Chodron says, "Never underestimate the urge to bolt." There was one participant who tried to leave in the wee hours of the morning on day two. Dawn, a member of our retreat management group, saw him walking out and jokingly asked, "You're not running away, are ya?"

And he replied, "Yes! Can I have my phone?" She was stumped and came and woke me up.

He and I spent some time talking and confronting what he was truly running away from. I told him that he could have his phone back right away, and whether he stayed or left was completely up to him. But I reminded him that if he left now, he was just repeating a pattern in his life. Here at the retreat, he had a safe space and group of people among whom he had an opportunity to see what was truly going on beneath the surface. Out in the real world, he wasn't going to have the same opportunity.

He decided to stay. He was very grateful that we had that conversation.

I myself can't remember how many times I wanted to bolt out of situations like this. There were times when I have said that enough is enough. *This is too painful; you can't make me do this.* I wanted to bolt from confronting the truth about where I was in my life. As the famous line from the movie *A Few Good Men* goes, "You can't handle the truth." I sure felt that way. I couldn't handle it. So when I see that terror show up in the eyes of my retreat participants, my heart goes out to them. I know how deeply painful it is to see yourself without the superficial safety of a veil. It's not easy. I have been there and gone through what I am asking them to go through. All I ask is that they trust me with this. They can make it. Healing is possible.

You too have the potential to not only heal from your past but also experience unconditional love and forgiveness. It's worth it. Just try it. Just trust what I am saying. Above all, trust in your innate potential and in your infinite ability to heal yourself. I am not healing you. I am just showing you how you can heal yourself.

And so I ask my retreat participants: If you were to pack your bags to set out on the best and most anticipated journey of your life, how would you pack? Bear in mind that this journey would lead you to that future authentic self, the truth and core of who you are. Would you pack the old, unwanted thoughts, emotions, and memories? Would you bring co-travelers along with you on this pious trip that didn't align with your vision of the authentic you? Would you carry anything at all that didn't serve the highest good of making this the most anticipated and best journey ever?"

I'm guessing that you probably wouldn't.

You might consider bringing with you the best of who you are: your truth, authenticity, talents, gifts, and passions. Right? You might consider choosing a guide, a co-traveler who gets who you are and lets you be you.

This makes all the sense in the world.

But how does one know what serves their highest good and what does not?

I think that we know this innately and can sense what serves us or doesn't. Acting on that inner knowing in our life may come easily to some, but most of us have to work on breaking old patterns and creating new ones, ones that are based in love—not in fear, pain, anger, or shame.

Some people say that deep down you have negative emotions and you have to deal with them so you can be happy, healed, and whole. But I think that deep down all we have is love. The negative emotions are just blocking our experience of that love, peace, and joy that are at the core of who we are.

When we do the I AM work in healing ourselves, we do the work of shedding the layers that we have draped on ourselves in an act of self-preservation. Due to negative experiences in our past, we have taken on different personas, avatars, belief systems, and thoughts so that we could counter the next affliction, attack, or abuse.

But now we are trying to heal. We are shifting now. The old way of thinking is not going to serve us in this new paradigm. The self is transforming and you are now creating new patterns in your life, patterns that will align with your highest good, help you use your true voice, tap into your inner power, and speak the unspeakable. You are moving away from the quagmire of your past. Now is your time to shine your inner light and experience liberation at the deepest level you ever have.

It's one thing to cope with newly emerging feelings at a retreat in a controlled environment: you are taken care of by a supporting group of people who "get" where you have been; you don't have to deal with the stress of everyday living; you know it's safe to say what you want to say. But what happens when you need to go back? How do you handle the triggers of people, places, flashbacks, and maybe even the very person responsible for violating you and causing your original trauma? I didn't realize at first that after the retreats I conducted for my participants, they were feeling the same way I had at my first retreat. As they said, "You've opened up this whole new world for us now; don't just leave us out in the wild—what do we have to do next to continue on this path?"

I really got it. You can't expect fruit from an apple tree by just planting a seed and not tending to it, watering it, fertilizing it. My own journey would have been rather different if I had not had the ongoing mentorship and guidance from my spiritual teachers and mentors. This is why the 11-month I AM Consciousness Program was such a good fit along with the retreat. Some participants were already in the yearlong program when they attended the retreat and some started the yearlong journey after experiencing the retreat.

When you arrive at the retreat, you enter a safe and sacred space where you can get present to who you are, what's really going with you, and how you feel about it. You experience meditations and exercises that help you release painful past memories, thoughts, and emotions that have been holding you back. A retreat participant once shared at the closing circle that she had come with a list of things that she had to work on herself for. She said that the moment the first session began, that list went flying out the window. She had never expected to be confronted with the fact that instead of her "issues" emerging that she had thought she needed to work on, the real issues revealed themselves as she started to become centered and present to herself.

During the retreat you practice a lot of silence. It is through the silence that you begin to listen more intentionally to your inner voice—your true voice—without judgment. Remember you're in a safe space. It is by being in this safe space that you can then gently begin the

After almost 15 years since my first experience of catharsis, I have learned that there is no single answer for everyone. We are all unique beings who have had unique experiences. We are all experiencing our own journeys, and that's a very personal thing. I can't begin to assume what your journey might be like. Your truth, your answer can come from only one place and one place alone—you.

But I know that I AM consciousness, you are consciousness, and together, we are the collective consciousness. What *you* are seeking is what is likely to create a cosmic convergence for *us*.

process of restoring, creating, and manifesting that which you would like to see happen in your life. You begin to see the possibility to have the life that you were purposed for, the life you were meant to live. You begin to see that light at the end of the tunnel. You see that light is within you. And once you connect with it, you know you have it in you to do it again and again. It is through the repeated submersion in the waters of this awareness and the practice of the meditations that this transformation happens. For a long time you may have seen yourself as a body full of pain, anger, and shame. You now begin to see that those were just layers, and they don't define who you truly are, and you can begin to perfect the new patterns of knowing, loving, and celebrating who you are.

Your future is waiting to embrace you with open arms. Meet it with love, compassion, and gratitude. Surrender to your divine potential and innate intelligence to heal yourself.

Today I am a living example that the potential for boundless healing is real. We all can heal together. All my retreat participants have taught me so much, helped me heal more with each retreat, and have been the inspiration for me to keep moving forward, growing this work, and even writing this book.

Since its inception, the I AM Retreat (formerly known as Anahatha Retreat) has offered a sacred and safe space for people to awaken, align, and act so that they can consciously and powerfully create a life they love. Over the years the retreats have had different themes, such as:

I AM Inner Power Retreat

I AM Love and Aliveness Retreat

I AM Self-Expression Retreat

I AM Abundance & Prosperity Retreat,

I AM Consciousness Retreat

People come in carrying heavy burdens, but they leave recharged, renewed, and ready to powerfully take on their life. Witnessing their transformation happen in front of my eyes is the most enlivening experience for me and why I am committed to offer these retreats. It was the hairpin bend in my life, and I know it can be for many others.

Private Mentoring

On a case-by-case basis, I still work with a small group of private clients. By leveraging technology, I can offer my support to clients over webinars, Google Hangouts, Skype, and the telephone. I have clients from all over the world, and I had always envisioned working with people in these ways. Sometimes I will have an extended private session with a client that is more like a personal one-on one retreat. Those are very powerful, but due to the amount of time they take, I do very few.

Group Mentoring

Group mentoring works very well. I have found that another participant's question will sometimes answer a question of mine that I never even knew I had. That's priceless. It also helps you see that you are not alone in your struggles, and it gives us perspective that even though we have our challenges, others do too, and we are all works in progress. Group mentoring is a great way of finding more clarity while still having the privacy to be on your own path of self-inquiry.

Transformative Techniques to Embrace

Unleash the Innate Power of the Body to Heal Using Your Breath

One of the most tangible tools of transformation that people find the simplest to get started with is the breath. You already know the significance of breath, the importance of deep breathing and the pitfalls of shallow breathing. What you might also know is that your state of mind, thoughts, and emotions considerably affect how you breathe. More stress, anxiety, and worry will result in superficial breathing. More peace, calm, and laughter will promote deep, conscious breathing. For as long as you are still breathing, know that you have an ally right there with you 24/7 at your service to help you heal. Like anything else, what you do with this information is up to you and when you are ready to get started.

What I learned when studying breath work through yoga, *siddha* (an ancient system of medicine from southern India), and other healing disciplines was that the breath (even laughter) could be used to activate deep-seated pockets of old memories, trauma, and emotions. Through different *mudras* or hand positions, one can rewire the circuitry of the breath and direct it to specific areas of the body, mind, and spirit. What seems like a physical practice turns into a deeply spiritual healing practice, and it's just using the breath. You are already breathing; why not practice conscious breathing for 10 or 15 minutes in your day and experience this powerful healing in your life?

The breath also has the ability to evoke feelings of unconditional love, forgiveness, and compassion. There are some breathing techniques that can help you raise or lower the temperature of your body based on the position of your tongue inside your mouth. In its very simplicity, the breath carries unwrapped gifts.

The first time I experienced "chaotic breathing" at a retreat, I thought everyone had gone mad. I really thought I was among lunatics and should run out of there. This is an exercise that involves forcefully pushing the breath out through the nostrils in an erratic and unpredictable manner. It can make you feel lightheaded and even nauseated, so please don't try this on your own. However, it was 10 minutes of this breathing that helped detonate the time bomb that was ticking inside me. The breath helped me explode like a volcano releasing all the lava filled with past anger, pain, and sadness. In the sessions that followed, I just kept allowing myself to be emptied of the toxic emotional waste as much as I could.

That was the storm before the calm. Then came a peaceful deep breath; then I was able to feel for the first time like I was fine, I was beautiful, I was lovable. The breath has an incredible capacity to heal. It is, for me, the most fundamental tool of transformation.

Unleash the Innate Power of the Mind to Heal Using Meditation

Participants sometimes ask me to teach them how to turn off their mind. "Help me just shut this thing down; it's driving me insane. Teach me a meditation or something so I can just check out for a few minutes and have some peace!"

The only way to shut the mind off that I am aware of is to be dead. I don't teach that. But first of all, to shut something off, don't you know need to where it is?

If I asked you, "Can you turn that light off, please? It's really glaring in my eyes," you would want to know where the switch is, right? You really want to help me, you want my eyes to stop hurting, you can see that I am uncomfortable—but where is the switch?

So let me ask you, this mind that you want to turn off, where is it? Some people answer it's your heart, your memory, or often, your brain. What else could it be? We see the mind as something corporeal because we believe what it tells us. It is so convincing; it states facts and presents radically extenuating evidence. How can it not be real? It is real. It has to be.

But it's not your brain. Your brain is your brain. The brain comprises the cerebral cortex, nerves, gray matter, medulla oblongata, and other tissues. The brain is material, tangible, physical. Your brain is not your mind. You think it is because the mind makes very intelligent and compelling arguments and the brain is the seat of your intelligence too; hence, the mind must be the brain. No.

OK, then, where is it?

Your mind is nonphysical, nonmaterial, intangible, and invisible. Untrained, it's like a yappy puppy just nipping away at his master's toes. It's annoying and that's why you want to shut it off. I get it. I would too. But the good news is that it can be trained. An unmanaged mind can wreak havoc on our breath, thoughts, feelings, and choices, and rob us of our wholeness in life. By training that puppy, the mind, we can experience harmony and healing.

The innate power of the mind is truly immense but mostly stays untapped. Through meditation, however, one can harness its energy and go from chaos to calm. I never thought there would come a day when I could experience any peace or calm in my mind. My mind was always running a million miles a minute—shuffling and shifting from pillar to post in frantic frenzy. Sometimes I look back and even I can't believe that was my life.

The transformation that happens with meditation lies in befriending the crazed mind, like training a wild horse. It takes patience and courage. Training a wild horse is a perilous task. Understanding the mind too can be daunting at first. It's almost like you have to wait for it to relieve itself of its lunacy. And then, when it begins to calm down, to just be with it. Letting it know everything is ok. You are an ally, not an adversary. It needs to hear from you so it can give up its need to be in control. The mind thinks, *If I don't take charge, then who will?*

When you create the space to have a conversation with yourself—that is, your mind—you can lay out the rules of engagement. You can say to your mind, "This is how this is going to work from now on. I know you have been telling me what to do all these years. I was in a lot of pain and anger and overwhelmed with the emotional residues of my past. You helped me get through that. I trained you to be afraid, have self-negating thoughts about us, and protect me from harm. Thank you for all that you have done for me.

"But I am here now. I can see how I have been holding myself back, and I am ready to move forward. There are going to be some changes in the way I do things and it's all for the better. Remember we are allies, not adversaries. We play on the same team, yes? This is going to be hard for you too. I am not going to listen to you when you give me advice based on the old way of life and thinking. I am changing, I am transforming. I am working toward manifesting a life that is aligned with my highest good. This is good for us, isn't it? I need you to work with me so that we can be happy and whole and live life to the fullest potential. I no longer want to define my life based on the stories of my past, so you have to stop repeating them to me, OK? Let's do this."

Like I say at my retreats, when the mind talks to you, talk back. Don't assume it knows what it's doing. Yappy pup, remember? Also know that you have the power to create your circumstances. With a few simple and basic meditations, you can start training the wild horses of your mind and experience clarity, peace, and miraculous healing.

I would also like to dispel the notion that to meditate is to sit in the lotus pose for an extended period of time staring at your navel. There are many ways to meditate and while sitting in the lotus pose could be one of them, it's not the one you might want to start with if you are new to meditation.

When I started, I couldn't even sit still for five minutes. I would open one eye to see if other students were as restless as I was. I would itch, scratch, and yawn. I had no focus, and sitting through 15 minutes of that, let alone 30, 40, or 60, was out of the realm of possibility.

Today I can meditate for two hours and it feels like five minutes have gone by. Granted, I don't get to spend two hours meditating every day, but when I do, it's bliss. You can gain so much with even 10 or 15 minutes of meditation if you allow yourself the time and space to make it happen. But only you can make it happen.

Our external environment will reflect where we are. Look around. Do you have the physical space for you? Are you living with old, unwanted objects and clutter in your life that don't serve your highest good anymore? Is looking after yourself a priority in your life? If so, what are you doing about it? Think about these things.

For the longest time my excuse was I didn't have a space to meditate. I looked around my house; we had a living and dining room, both of which were never used. We had a family room for the family, a playroom for the kids. We had a library from which to work, a kitchen, and bedrooms. Over 3,000 square feet of living space, but I just couldn't find a two-by-two spot to sit my ass down and close my eyes for 15 minutes. Bullshit, right?

I have made all the excuses in the world to not sit and meditate. I'll do it later, I just ate, I have my period, I have too much to do—the list is endless. When you start practicing, you will see for yourself. But when I do get down to it, it's just wonderful. Now I can always tell when I am trying to justify my excuses, and over the years I have gotten better at calling myself out when I am trying to bullshit myself. It works most times. Sometimes, well, I still have those blind spots . . .

The irony is that after losing the aforementioned house to the bank, downsizing to under 2,000 feet with a growing family, making one-tenth of the money I used to, I was finally able to start meditating even more deeply. Suddenly, even in a house half the size of the one before, I was somehow able to create the space and dedicate an entire room to my meditation practice. What I learned from this was the space I created in my life to pause was not directly proportionate to the space in my home but more closely related to the space I held within me. It was more to do with the bandwidth I had emotionally and mentally to pause. Whether I have a beautiful space or not was completely dependent on me. And I know that it is a reflection of the space I have cleared within me.

But it's not just about having a meditation room in my house. I still have to open the door, enter the room, sit down, and meditate. That takes practice. That's why it's called a meditation practice—because you have to . . . practice.

Zig Ziglar's quote about motivation and bathing is the perfect way to illustrate what happens when you meditate one time and expect everything to be different. It is because the effects of "meditation" (like motivation) fade away that I recommend you start a meditation practice, not just seek instant gratification and drive-through breakthroughs or casual weekend "spa-and-wine" type experiences at retreats—although they have their own place. If you want to create a sustainable course to healing in your life, then I strongly recommend that you consider making meditation a part of it. You don't expect to keep running your car after it's out of gas, do you? Even if it's an electric car, you need to charge it. You don't expect to never brush your teeth or to visit the dentist every six months yet be in the hall of fame for the best set of pearly whites ever, do you?

The effects of meditation are cumulative. Some days you might feel like you had an incredible meditation and some days it might feel ordinary. You can't fully predict how a meditation will leave you feeling or what insights you might have during it. Being attached to the outcome takes you away from the simplicity and ease of meditation. Just breathe, relax, and practice being present: that—allowing yourself to be in the moment—is meditation. I will say it again: The effects of meditation are cumulative. Every time you meditate, whether it's for 20 minutes or five seconds, you are adding positive units to your wholeness. Meditation is your portal to go from the ordinary to the extraordinary. Why not give yourself that gift?

Once the most mischievous wild horses and yappy dogs could be tamed in my mind, I was able to uncover new insights about my journey.

Those insights have furthered my healing and transformation; hence, I am forever grateful that I did not give up. I tried every excuse in the book to not have to meditate, but the rewards of meditation have far outweighed the practice's perceived inconvenience.

It was during one of my meditations 15 years after I first began that I understood my dysfunctional relationship with food. I believe my problem with overeating began the day my mother gave me the huge responsibility of keeping a terrible secret.

"Never tell anyone, OK, Richa?"

I had just been given permission to lie, to be deceptive, by the one person who had taught me my whole life to never tell lies, to always be truthful, and that honesty is the best policy.

Suddenly I had this warped sense of power and control. I could lie. Well, if I could lie about one thing, then I could cover up even more stuff, couldn't I? How about if I don't want to study for my chemistry exam; can I just copy from someone? Let me try. And so I did. I didn't get caught. Let me try it again. I tried it on my physics exams. I took the entire guide—the compilation of all the CliffsNotes of the entire year's curriculum including specific answers and diagrams—into the exam hall. I got caught. It was not pleasant.

Still, I lied about everything I could. I lied to my principal after I got caught that my parents were beating me up at home. I told the school that I had a stepmother although one look at my mother and me would prove we are related; I am the spitting image of her.

At one point in my school life, we moved to different cities. In elementary school in the first city, my brother and I were ahead of our class and were moved up a year, and so I skipped first grade. When we moved, however, he had to repeat the sixth grade and I the fifth grade. It was all OK until we moved back. I guess my brother didn't care and was upfront with his friends, but I felt so concerned about being "behind" by a year that I lied to my friends when I got back by telling them I was in the same grade as they were. We were in different schools so they didn't find out. On the weekends, we would hang out, have sleepovers, and watch movies together, and the whole time they didn't know that I was a year behind them at school. Technically, though, I wasn't "behind"—but admitting that I was in terms of my grade level felt like a stigma in a society where there was all this pressure to be academically superior.

Lying had become my survival technique. Any tough situation? I would lie my way out of it. I was told I could. My own mother had given me permission to be a liar. So why not use this to my advantage?

As I said, it was during one of my meditations that I realized it was right after my mother asked me to keep our big secret that I started overeating. I was a tomboy growing up. I played a lot of sports and was very active. I had an 18-inch waist and I could wear anything I wanted. I was taking ballet and tennis and was on the school basketball team. But in the ninth grade, I dropped out of all the extracurricular activities and started putting on weight, sitting at home more depressed than ever. I felt like I was walking on eggshells all the time at home. I know my mother didn't see the connection between what she had asked of me that day and the radical changes I was exhibiting, and neither did I.

My ballet teacher wrote to my parents saying what a good dancer I was and requested that I come back. My tennis coach implored my dad to not let me drop out. My parents asked me if I was sure that I wanted to stop. I said yes and that was that. They weren't like some other parents who just don't listen to what their children want and literally force them into taking up a sport because they love it so much themselves.

My parents were convinced they were doing the right thing, I know, but they were unable to look beneath the surface to connect the dots. I loved dancing and playing tennis. I really wish I hadn't dropped out. But at the time I was unable to carry the weight of thriving at those things while growing up in a dysfunctional family.

The meditation helped me understand that the energetic residue of these episodes in my life had lodged a belief that I would never finish what I started. I had believed that I was a jack-of-all-trades and master of none, which caused me to doubt my ability to make decisions, to fight my instincts, and to mistrust my gut more times than I would have liked. But once it became apparent to me that that was what I was doing, I knew I had an opportunity to redress the situation, rephrase my inner dialog, harness the wild horses, train that puppy.

And so, through a mindful and consistent meditation practice, I was able to melt away some of those hard-to-face, deeply wedged old belief systems of the past that were still lingering within me. If you were to only unwrap that gift, the practice of meditation and its cumulative effect could deliver to you illuminating joy each day.

Unleash the Innate Power of the Spirit to Heal Using Silence

We are trained since childhood to be polite, speak nicely, and say the right things that are politically correct. I don't believe there is anything wrong in doing those things. What I feel we may have missed was learning the significance of sometimes not saying anything at all—the significance of silence.

I remember that through my adolescent years and until my transformation work began, I hated silence. All I could hear were the nasty voices in my head that were putting me down, reminding me of the shame, guilt, and anger that were brewing within me. *You are dirty, filthy, nobody likes you. You caused this to happen to you. You invited it.* I was not comfortable hearing this commentary, so I had to somehow drown it out, make it go away. I would try to keep myself extremely busy, turn the music on at a very high volume, close the door, dance until I was exhausted, and exist in a haze, trying to be convinced that my life was all right. This strategy, coupled with drinking and smoking, was not incredibly wholesome!

But through catharsis, meditation, and transformation work, I was able to clear my mind and arrive at a place of serenity and silence for the first time. I remember being with myself in a room and feeling calm and quiet. I felt like I could have a peaceful conversation with myself. It was like meeting a long-lost friend and catching up with her. Like Mia in *Pulp Fiction*, I felt like I could "comfortably enjoy the silence." I had never felt that way before.

When we practice silence, we conserve our energy. We build up a reservoir of inner power and strength by saying nothing. On the other hand, we deny ourselves the innate power of silence by thinking we need to keep up with the energy other people bring to our space—gossip, to which we are expected to listen and contribute; anger from rude or obnoxious others who want to pick a fight; telephone calls we don't want to answer but do so anyway just to be polite; and then, of course, the multitude of electronic gizmos and digital distractions that add to our interruption-driven lifestyle. All of these rob us of opportunities for silence too.

If you ask me, I think that caller ID is one of the best inventions of our times. It allows you to choose to *ignore* intrusions. No one says you have to answer the phone if you don't want to. In the same way, you can choose to claim the silence that you want and need in your life. The question is—are you really ready for it?

If you are afraid to be with your own mind and thoughts right now, that's understandable. You can begin to practice silence in simpler ways than going cold turkey. There are multiple times during the day when you have the opportunity to practice silence and may not even realize it. A drive to the store or a cup of tea on the front porch represents a basic day-to-day activity during which you might claim a few moments of silence. You may try using a timer and sit in silence for as little as three, five, or seven minutes. You will find yourself wanting to add more time to stay still in your own skin as you become more comfortable. Take the time you need to do that and be gentle with yourself.

One of the I AM Retreat guidelines is, "Give yourself permission to be in silence." We do practice silence in retreats but also have sessions in which there is an opportunity for participants to discuss and share. The importance of instituting silence as a core practice for inner awareness is to bring our focus back to ourselves. Banal dialogue and polite conversations keep our focus turned outward. When silence is the norm for a defined period of time, then your attention is turned inward. The direction of the flow of your thoughts changes and becomes more focused and clear. You begin to notice where you are, how you are, and how you feel about that. No one is asking that you go to a 15-day all-silent retreat right off the bat, but if that is the type of experience that will get you to truly experience silence at a deep level, then go for it!

For some people, silence can be very challenging. It's like putting the brakes on an 18-wheel truck that's speeding down the highway at 100 miles an hour. That truck is going to take some time to slow down, let alone come to a complete stop. That's how we are moving in life—we are just bolting down that highway. Even though we know intellectually that we should probably take a pause, we say, "One more thing, just one more thing, and then I will . . ." Been there, done that.

Needless to say, during a silent retreat it takes most participants the first day to unwind. The silence seems very uncomfortable, and I can see them trying to make eye contact with other participants or sneaking around the corner of the cabin to say something to someone. My team will report back to me, and sometimes I feel like that participant may

Desiderata
by Max Ehrmann, 1927

Go placidly amid the noise and haste, and remember what
peace there may be in silence.

As far as possible without surrender be on good terms with
all persons.

Speak your truth quietly and clearly; and listen to others,
even the dull and ignorant; they too have their story.

Avoid loud and aggressive persons, they are vexations to
the spirit.

If you compare yourself with others, you may become vain
and bitter;

for always there will be greater and lesser persons than
yourself.

Enjoy your achievements as well as your plans.

Keep interested in your career, however humble; it is a real
possession in the changing fortunes of time.

Exercise caution in your business affairs; for the world is full of
trickery.

But let this not blind you to what virtue there is; many persons strive for high ideals;

and everywhere life is full of heroism.

Be yourself.

Especially, do not feign affection.

Neither be critical about love; for in the face of all aridity
and disenchantment it is as perennial as the grass.

Take kindly the counsel of the years, gracefully surrendering
the things of youth.

Nurture strength of spirit to shield you in sudden misfortune.
But do not distress yourself with imaginings.

Many fears are born of fatigue and loneliness. Beyond a
wholesome discipline, be gentle with yourself.

You are a child of the universe, no less than the trees and
the stars;

you have a right to be here.

And whether or not it is clear to you, no doubt the universe
is unfolding as it should.

Therefore be at peace with God, whatever you conceive
Him to be,

and whatever your labors and aspirations, in the noisy
confusion of life keep peace with your soul.

With all its sham, drudgery and broken dreams, it is still a
beautiful world. Be cheerful.

Strive to be happy.

need a reminder, but other times I think, *Let me see where this goes*. It all depends on the who, the what, and the why in the moment.

And then come the mealtimes. Just before our first dinner together, I make an announcement and then add, "And just a reminder, we will be eating in silence." I see the look on their faces change. Smiles generally appear on their faces right after I say, "Dinner is ready" and disappear right after I announce "Silence." I see some confusion, some resentment, and also some anger now and again. It's as if the participants are saying they understand practicing silence while taking a nature hike or being introspective, but why do they have to be punished during dinner? This is crazy!

Punish . . . yes, punish. That's what we think silence is—punishment. That's what perhaps some of us learned as children. We were punished by being sent to our room or being taught it wasn't polite to talk a certain way or were grounded for speaking out inappropriately. We were shamed into our silence. Silence was not a celebration; it was a punishment. So I understand the "Why do you have to punish us?" question all too well.

Sandy, an older participant at a retreat, once took me aside and shared with me the following:

"I remember eating dinner in utter silence when I was a little girl. The only sound in the house was of my mother being thrashed by my father in the other room. My sisters and I would be eating at the table and listening to the sounds of the beating and my mother howling. And then they would come and join us for dinner like nothing had happened. She would serve him his dinner plate and then talk to us about school."

When Sandy ate in silence, it reminded her of her father. She thought that at any minute, her mother might come flying across the kitchen table or be flung onto the refrigerator. Silence was an unsafe place to be, it was threatening. As a little girl, she formed a belief that when she was in silence, something really horrible was happening, and to prevent or avoid it, she had to drown out the silence as much as she could.

Our talking together helped her get present in the moment and see that, first of all, she was in a safe space. She now had the opportunity to confront her past of being a witness to her father's rage: his physical, mental, and emotional abuse of her mother, herself, and her siblings. During the meditation the next morning, she released, for the first time in her life, 50 years of suppressed, unspoken, unexpressed feelings and emotion. She felt that an elephant had been lifted off of her chest.

Though the initial phase of getting quiet was testing for Sandy, she stayed with the process and came out having a positive experience. By the third day, most participants have begun to experience what a "comfortable silence" is.

But to return to the issue of silence during mealtimes for a moment. Why is that important? We spend so much time, energy, and money on buying groceries, preparing meals, and then getting them on the table for one meal. When we sit down to eat, we are usually distracted by the TV, smart phones, and mundane chitchat. Of course some meaningful and intentional communication happens during meals when you are at home. But at the retreat, we like that you experience the mindfulness and inner awareness that comes with eating your food in silence. In the silence you get to listen to what your taste buds are saying to you. You get to truly sense the flavors, textures, and temperature of the food that might otherwise be absent from your experience. If every meal you had was just like every other spent in chitchat and conversation, you would not have this opportunity to experience what silent-eating meditation is like. You always have permission to be silent; the question is, how often do you claim it for yourself? At the retreat, we want you to just focus on you. Don't worry if participants need something; the team is there to support them. Or let them help themselves. You help yourself and focus on you.

Take time to be fully present to what you are eating, how much you are eating, how the food tastes, how the texture feels in your mouth, and how these perceptions make you feel overall. Are you turning to food to stuff your emotions? Are you eating to feel better? Noticing these nuances at mealtime help you get present to hidden patterns of emotional and compulsive eating. So take the time to notice what needs noticing. Think about these introspective questions and see where those thoughts lead you. In silence, you allow yourself to have insights that are not easy to have otherwise.

You are met where you are. When you are ready, silence will feel natural, normal, organic. Like any other practice or tool for transformation, silence cannot be coerced. Silence is an invitation to your sanctum sanctorum, the deepest, most precious part of you, your inner sanctuary. When you practice silence, you energize your spirit and refuel your inner power. You are able to unleash the innate power of your spirit to create opportunities for deeper healing. Silence has been called golden, and as a tool for healing, it is invaluable.

The Guidelines

Over the past 15 years and several conversations, lectures, seminars, and coaching sessions with clients and students about transformation, healing, and success, I have found the following themes emerge to form a set of retreat guidelines that apply again and again:

1. **It's OK to not be OK**

   Embrace every situation as it is, whether you think it's what you want or not. After all, resisting a situation will never change it, but it will always make you less comfortable. Embracing a situation without resistance will allow you to bypass the state of denial and move forward on the solid ground of reality. You can see the situation for what it is, not worse than it is, and you are free from the devastating effects of self-pity. Self-pity influences the way you talk to yourself, your internal dialogue.

   When driving down the street, for example, you may end up behind an unreasonably slow driver. You have somewhere important to be, and they are driving 10 miles under the speed limit. Against your good sense, your natural inclination is to start slipping into frustration and adopt a mental attitude and emotional state that works against you. You may notice the words inside your head cursing the slow driver and the situation, or asking, "Why does something always make me late?" Besides the fact that this negative mental chatter keeps you from having productive thoughts and feeling positive feelings, focusing on the negative, and resisting it, sends you on a downward spiral.

   On the other hand, when you can learn to be okay with things not going your way and take control of the only thing you have control of, yourself, you can make a hugely positive impact on your life. I created a video course titled 11 Secrets to an Empowered Life to dive much deeper into exactly how you can go beyond understanding this principle and learn to really implement it in your daily life. Imagine the impact this one principle could have in your life if you really put it to use!

2. Give yourself permission to be in silence

How can silence help us have a more fulfilled life? While many of us have developed a negative view of silence and solitude, consciously or subconsciously, silence, when embraced and cherished, can be one of your most rewarding experiences. The ability to allow yourself to sit in silence expands your self-awareness and allows you to make deep contact with more of who you are.

If silence can be so beneficial for personal growth, peace of mind, and overall happiness, why do so many of us seem to avoid it? As a child, were you ever told to be quiet and go to your room? Being alone became a punishment, and loneliness developed as we felt we were losing out on something. If you feel like something is missing when it's quiet or you have trouble being alone without feeling lonely, you may just be living out your prior programming and missing a deeper connection with yourself.

As adults, or "grown children," we need to take it upon ourselves to reprogram ourselves intentionally. Silence is a wondrous part of life that opens us up to greater understanding, allows us to realize higher levels of inner peace, and increases our sense of direction in life. In this, too, the 11 Secrets to an Empowered Life video can show you exactly how you can practice intentional silence in order to reprogram yourself with empowering beliefs and open yourself up to a whole new world of possibilities.

3. Feel everything

This one can seem a bit counterintuitive, especially if you've been taught the power of "positivity." You might wonder if feeling pain, sadness, anger, and grief would slow you down from attaining joy, peace, happiness, and love. Actually, pretending that your pain is not there is like pretending your house isn't on fire. If you really convince yourself, you may feel a bit better for a little while, but before long, you've got to address the issue.

The fastest and, really, the only way to truly move on from past hurts and embrace the joy and peace of the moment is to feel your pain fully. The same door that keeps out pain keeps out joy. You have to open the door up to everything to experience true authentic happiness. If you are still haunted by past events, then chances are you never really felt them fully. In order to move on with your life, you have to allow yourself to feel the pain wholly and honestly. You will be rewarded with an immense sense of clarity and freedom.

In the guided meditation in the video, I go over the step-by-step process you can use to cleanse your emotional body of baggage and past hurts and regain your ability to live fully in the present moment, joyfully wielding your full power.

4. **Be in the here and now**

Being fully present is what life is really all about. But so often, we end up stuck in the past or the future, mentally and emotionally, only leaving our physical bodies to live in the present. We seem to think that "someday" will be the day when we are at peace, enjoying the moment, and having the time of our lives, if we could just get this next pay raise, this new house, and so on.

The unfortunate truth is that for so many, the day when they can live fully in the moment and really appreciate all the wonder of life right before their eyes never comes. The truth is that life will never be "just right," no matter how good it gets. There is always something more to do, have, and be. When we learn to love that element of life, we can relax in the moment, be with our loved ones, our children, our friends and spouses, and be even more effective in our professions and life endeavors. When we live in the moment, every day becomes a truly fulfilling day.

5. **Acknowledge who you are**

"Know thyself." These famous words from ancient Greek philosophers encompass a huge portion of what it means to be a whole human being. Acknowledging who and what you are, and why you are who you are, means that you accept and embrace every aspect of yourself: the good, the bad, and the ugly.

We all have our strengths and we all have our weaknesses, and understanding what those are for each of us is what sets us free to be who we are, unabashedly, and love every second of it. When you know who you truly are, you can align yourself with that image and live to your greatest potential. Authenticity gives you greater power and also a greater sense of inner peace.

The good news is that you don't have to do this perfectly in one shot to experience the benefits of being in alignment with yourself. There are little moves that you can make to know yourself better, and accept all that you are.

6. **Understand that you are a spiritual being having a human experience**
   What is spiritual and what is spirituality? We as humans often seek spirituality and spiritual things when, in truth, everything has a spiritual element. We are already pure spirit. A weekend spiritual retreat will not make us spiritual, and 20 books on spirituality won't either. Embrace the fact that you are in full contact with spirit here and now.

   Take a breath. You are feeling spirit flow through your body. Listen to the sounds around you. You are hearing the voice of spirit manifest physically. There is so much magic all around us to be taken in, to be cherished and enjoyed every single second. But when we get caught up in our mundane tasks, stress, and the mind-numbing day-to-day grind, we lose contact with this magical element of life bit by bit.

   You are not your body, you are not your clothes, you are not your job, you are not even your personality. All these things are passing, but there is an element of you that is eternal, that is expansive and infinite—the spirit within you. Embracing and contacting this part of you will give you all the inspiration, power, belief, and direction you need to be everything you are meant to be.

7. **Do less and be more**
   Busy, action-oriented, even boring activities dominate most people's lives. Then once the mindless daily grind is over, we numb ourselves with television, a few glasses of wine, and drift off into sleep, just to awaken and do it all over tomorrow, day after day, until years have gone by. Many people never escape the hypnotic loop and end up dying before they ever really live.

   Not a pretty picture, and I don't believe that's in store for you. The fact that you are reading this tells me that you aren't the type to settle for less than you can be, or the type to lose sight of what's really important. Doing less and being more means that you refuse to engage in the meaningless, humdrum activities that eat up your time and energy.

   Allow yourself the space to grow and *be* more, and you'll find that as you become more, the things that you *do* become more powerful. You have leverage from the point of being; the more you *are*, the more meaningful everything you *do* becomes.

8. **Remember that the question is the answer**

Asking a question is an immediate invitation to your subconscious mind to find the answer. A question and its answer are intimately connected. This is a powerful concept, and a powerful truth. This one secret, if understood and used, could change your life forever. If a question and an answer are directly linked to each other, any answer can be found by asking the right question. *The right question.*

I put extra emphasis on that phrase because the concept of "ask and it is given" is a double-edged sword. If you ask a good question, you get a good answer. If you ask a bad question, you get a bad answer. If people ask, "Why can't I do it?" their subconscious mind will unerringly retrieve a buffet of reasons why they can't do it. If they ask, "How can I make it happen?" they are now back on the path to getting what they want.

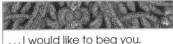

...I would like to beg you, dear Sir, as well as I can, to have patience with everything unresolved in your heart and to try to love the questions themselves as if they were locked rooms or books written in a very foreign language. Don't search for the answers, which could not be given to you now, because you would not be able to live them. And the point is to live everything. Live the questions now. Perhaps then, someday far in the future, you will gradually, without even noticing it, live your way into the answer.

—Rainer Maria Rilke,
in *Letters to a Young Poet*

Listen to the questions you ask yourself. Are you asking the right questions in the right way? The big questions, like *Who am I, really?* and *What will my life mean?* are often pushed out of the way because they seem more complex and daunting. But when you just open yourself up to the questions, with patience and an open mind, the answers will be drawn to you, unfolding in just the perfect way for you.

9. **Be aware that your words are the vessel of your day**

Just as a vessel gives shape to the water it holds, your words give shape to your life, your day, and your destiny. Words are the language of your mind. They are the filters through which you interpret the world. The words you say to others and the words you say to yourself determine how your life will turn out.

Words make up ideas, and ideas make up your philosophy. The way you think about life, about yourself, about the events and the people you encounter determine what course of action you will take and the results that you will have. The words that go through your head throughout the day are a clear picture of what is really going on in your subconscious mind. And if you listen closely, you can see the patterns and understand why you get what you get in life.

We learn our habits of speech and thought as children, and for many of us, the longer we continue to use the same ideas, phrases, and language patterns, the less flexible we feel to change. But luckily, habits can be reprogrammed just as easily as they can be set in the first place, and in the 11 Secrets video course, I teach you exactly how you can reprogram your mind for success using the power of the words you say to yourself and to others.

10. **I am consciousness. You are consciousness. We are the collective consciousness**

Ancient religions have long known, and modern science now knows, that everything is connected. That is significant because it means that everything also affects everything. Our physical world of seemingly separate items is actually made up of energy in motion, vibrations. Everything is what it is because of the frequency of its vibration. A chair is a chair, light is light, and your life is what it is because of the state of your vibration. As humans we are in a very special position, because our thoughts produce an energetic vibration that impacts the world we live in and everyone around us. This is how the law of attraction works. We use our thoughts and emotions to create an energetic field.

None of us has a separate world to live in. We all affect one another. It is our responsibility to own our vibrational state and be fully accountable for what we are manifesting for ourselves and those around us. Our decisions, attitudes, and state of awareness are a responsibility as much as they are powers for us to wield. In the 11 Secrets video, I show you how you can use all of this to your benefit by raising your vibrational levels and "tuning" yourself for success and happiness.

11. **Be in the attitude of gratitude**

Gratitude makes hard things easier, good things better, and life more enjoyable. There are also more specific benefits to gratitude, one of which is its snowball effect. This means that when you are grateful for what you have and where you are, you can see the good, and you focus on it. And when you focus on the good things, you tune yourself to see and create more good things in your life, and the effect is that you gain momentum in a positive direction and generate more and more of what you want.

Living with an attitude of gratitude for the present moment will create a sort of bubble—a protective field around you that keeps out negative thoughts and emotions. You may find that negative people will either be more positive around you or be unwilling to enter your space at all. When you focus intensely on the good and celebrate it with positive emotions, you leave no place for negativity in your life.

Holding yourself in a state of gratitude is a process. Like any habit, it takes time and persistence, but the life you can live with gratitude is worth every effort. In the 11 Secrets video, I teach you exactly how you can implement a lasting attitude of gratitude.

12. **Allow no inner judgments, criticism, or opinions**

Your energy is your most valuable resource. Don't waste it on inner commentary. Thank the critic and gently encourage that voice to take a back seat.

The brain cannot always distinguish between what you think vs. what is real. The more you dwell on negative thinking, the more likely your brain is going to perceive those negative thoughts as reality. Then, perhaps without your conscious awareness, you will integrate those thoughts into your self-perception, and your feelings and perhaps even behavior will change in accordance with your worsening self-image.

For this reason alone, it is important to keep your mind as free as possible from negative thoughts about yourself. At the very least, you can avoid digging the trenches of negativity deeper than they already may be.

13. Speak the unspeakable

Take a moment to bring hidden secrets out from within you and express what you have not yet expressed. If it works for you to write, then write. If it works for you to talk to someone, then talk to someone. If there is another way that works best for you, then do that. But take action to get the unsaid said and get out of denial.

Unfortunately, thoughts and memories kept locked inside, especially ones that you feel are shameful or painful, gain power. It's as if the very act of suppressing them strengthens them. Verbalizing them, writing them down, or somehow finding a way to uncage them from your brain allows you to look at them more objectively and see them for what they are: merely "things" that happened to you, things that may have led you to take certain actions or behave in a certain way that you might now regret. But by getting them outside yourself and staring them down, you are robbing them of power. You've seen and experienced their worst, so they can't continue to hurt you with the energy they initially had.

Challenging denial by getting it out on the table in front of you is profoundly empowering. Remember: you are not alone, others have endured what you have endured, and the isolation you might feel as a result of your negative experiences often has more to do with your *choosing* to isolate your experiences from others. Share the unspeakable, get it outside of yourself, even if—at first—it's "only" onto a piece of paper or your computer.

6

The Possibilities

In the past, I had such a low opinion of myself, I didn't feel like I was worth anything. I felt I was only good for being exploited. I was always looking for possibilities—an escape or a monumental change in my life—for a way out from what was plaguing me, whether plotting to commit a murder or to run away. The day I saw that I could shift from the possibility of prostitution to the possibility of peace, however, the rules of the game changed.

At first I saw only limited possibilities, such as when I was offered the role of Stella in *A Streetcar Named Desire*. This was just two years after my move to New Delhi, after I had left home. Over break between semesters, I read the play and just knew I *had* to be Blanche DuBois. Blanche was Stella's older sister who had a dreadful past and was swiftly losing her mind. I saw myself in Blanche because, like her, I felt I was crumbling, hiding behind a veneer of social snobbery and sexual righteousness. Blanche and I were both insecure, dislocated, and on a path that was no more than a descent into insanity. I believed that if I played Blanche, I could perhaps slow my fall and vicariously help heal my own trauma.

But instead of coming clean and speaking what was unspeakable, being honest with my teacher, the legendary Mr. Ebrahim Alkazi, I turned down the role of Stella because I was disheartened and unsettled that I hadn't been chosen to play Blanche. So I refused to be in the play altogether and moved out of town—again. I made the compelling argument of needing to move to Bombay both because that was where Sid was headed and because that's where all actors and actresses go to realize their silver-screen dreams. When one door closes, another one opens. I saw new possibilities for myself in Bombay.

No one questioned my logic, and my parents acquiesced to my request as they were growing fond of the idea that if Sid and I were serious, we would marry, thus reducing their social burden, in a sense. No matter how shallow and superficial, marrying one's daughter off was, and still is, a major yardstick in Indian culture for measuring societal acceptance and commanding respect.

My time in New Delhi was over. My drama teacher was disappointed that I was leaving the group, and it broke my heart that my decision saddened him. But I could not speak my truth—that playing a role in *Streetcar* would have been traumatic for me. I was afraid I might come undone; the best solution was to just escape the setting altogether and fly away. It may have been therapeutic for me to actually have been in the production, and perhaps it even may have been the turning point I needed in my life, but it was not meant to be.

I did not realize then that what I *thought* I was doing for all the right reasons was just my way of preserving myself. I did not have the tools to expose my wounds, to be open about my pain, anger, shame, and sadness. I lacked the courage to be vulnerable, and I wasn't going to risk exposing again the secret I'd been sworn to keep. But after I started healing and doing the transformation and meditation work, I began to see a glimmer of hope, rays of light more often. I was able to taste for the first time something other than shame and anger. I was able to taste hope and love.

When I ran out of energy and felt like I was getting weak again, I knew where I could go to recharge and refuel myself. Over time I had developed my own support system to cope with the ups and downs of my journey, so I always came back to the energy, healing, meditation, and introspection. These tools for transformation consistently helped me, no matter what came my way. Truthfully, sometimes my response to adversity would be delayed. I would most certainly fall back into the old "poor me" pattern. But I refused to dwell in despair for too long, and sooner or later I would realize that there was something wrong with that approach and I needed to do something about it.

I received many interesting reactions when I first started talking to others about writing this book. Of course my closest friends were completely supportive. They had been waiting for years for me to finally write it. Others, however, looked at me like I was naïve and living in a fool's paradise.

When I began writing, my father was fully participating in my life and in the lives of my children. When I told this to others, I would hear comments like, "Your father is in your life, really? You let him see your daughters? Wow, that's a good story." I wondered why some people were being so suspicious of our reconciliation. *Do they think it is too good to be true? Am I missing something? Have I really forgiven, or am I just pretending so that I can move on with my life?* I shrugged off these doubts because what I felt was true for me; my father and I had come a long way, and our efforts to do so had been genuine.

"Your parents never separated? Your mother continued to stay with him? That's unbelievable," they would say. Again, I would have doubts and fears flash through my mind and heart. *But I have done the work, I have forgiven, I have self-expressed myself—what more is needed of me? Why do some people find this so hard to digest? Do my healing and transformation look like an act or do they look fabricated? But I feel whole and good about this, and that's what matters above all. I am good with this. This is my truth.* And again, I would reset myself, never doubting that I had made the best decision in my life. I was living a life of possibility with optimism as my religion. I felt strong.

At times, though, it felt like these inquisitive questioners were not outside of me. Could they be aspects of my own subconscious? Such reflections continued to help me with my self-awareness. *Have I really forgiven my dad? Have I genuinely, unconditionally, forgiven him? Or is it because I want to believe that healing is possible, that I am healed, that we all have the potential to do so, and that there is hope in this world for one and all—and that there is hope for my children and their children?*

It was for these reasons and, yes, doubts that I finally made my choice. I firmly believed by this time on my journey that if I did not break my silence by writing this book and telling my story, the malaise that arises from any repressed feelings of shame, rage, and sadness within me would erupt throughout the rest of the days of my life, destroying my optimistic spirit, rendering me powerless to fully serve others or share my understanding of life's lessons. I also believed that if I remained in a state of limbo, this malaise would undoubtedly proliferate in the generations to come, somehow seeping osmotically through my emotional, mental, and spiritual cell walls to be absorbed by my daughters—sickness transmitted to the next generation. I could not bear to look the other way and pretend that I did not have a responsibility to heal myself. This mattered. I could no longer honor my mother's gag order. I could no longer hold sacred my parents' reputation in their communities at the cost of suffocating my children's future.

There was a time that life seemed like it would be filled with an eternal darkness. But during that one morning, on the day of my first transformation retreat with Prema, I found a little hope, a glimmer, as from a firefly's spark of light. I clung to that little firefly in the darkness of the night and held onto the hope that one day, maybe one day, I would climb out of this deep well of despair. And I did, one slippery rung of a ladder at a time. I did what I could with what I knew at the time and when I knew it. I lived my life to my fullest potential with what I had to work with. I was met where I was, and that one little firefly lifted me through gradually ebbing shades of darkness to bring me into the light.

I began to see new possibilities. I saw that there was a possibility for peace. I saw that there was a possibility to tap my latent talent. I saw that there was a possibility to be free of my past. I saw that there was a possibility to heal, love, and forgive unconditionally. I saw that there was a possibility to be compassionate.

Reviewing other leading books on the subject of healing from sexual abuse, I saw that compassion and forgiveness were not really stressed. I don't believe it is the responsibility of those who have been abused as children to take it upon themselves to force compassion and forgiveness within themselves, to feel compelled to move on or to forget. That would be just another way to guilt someone into doing what's right for others at the cost of doing what's wrong for you. However, I do invite them to do the work, to feel everything, to know that "It's OK to not be OK" and to see themselves as already perfect, just the way they are. I also believe that when the time is right, when they are ready, unconditional love, compassion, and forgiveness would be the second greatest gift they will receive. The first gift would be meeting themselves for who they are, complete in every way—like coming home to the heart and finding it a warm, loving place.

And so, to reaffirm what I said at the beginning of the Preface to this book: I think that it *is* possible to heal from childhood sexual abuse. I think I can look back and say that all the work I have done in healing my past has been fruitful. It has helped me be a good mother, wife, teacher, and daughter. The healing has helped me bring a good energy into this world. I believe in myself, in my work, what I have to provide to this planet in my lifetime. I feel good about those things, really good. I love who I am, who I have become. I am not sure that at 42—my age as I write this—I would have had the clarity of my higher purpose in this life had I not used these very tools for my own transformation. My life could have gone in many different directions, and I am glad that I picked this one. I am really glad.

Be the Change

While there are a lot of great things happening in the world and even in our own lives, we can't deny the presence of strife, disappointment, and unhappiness that exist all around us. But we adapt, learn, and cope with our pain and difficulties and give everything we have to succeed despite our history. Many leave their burdens behind them, in the past, where they belong. Many trek through life carrying their burdens, unnecessarily, the entire way. While a degree of success and happiness does arrive, it often brings with it ominous reminders every time of what was sacrificed for this achievement, and so there is an echo that lingers from the shadows of our past.

If we are to create an authentically joyous and happy life with where we are right now, this moment, then we need to release, to let go of, the past and all its shadows. Our life is a mere reflection of our state of inner being. As goes our inner happiness, so goes the happiness in our life. In order to see happiness manifest in our life, we must exude happiness from within.

So the question comes down to: Are we being the change we want to see in the world?

We wish for peace in the world, but do we have inner peace?

We wish for our children to manifest their fullest potential, but are we manifesting ours?

We wish for humanity to be kind, loving, and forgiving of one another, but are we able to be kind, loving, and forgiving to the people in our own life?

Are we willing to give permission to ourselves to create a future of love, possibility, and joy? Can we sow the seeds for this future while withholding fresh air and water but still expect the fruits?

How are we to have a world that has healed if we are still hurting? Without our healing, each of our healing, the world still remains in pain. Even if my little toe is in pain, I am in pain. If I burn my hand, I hurt everywhere. If I pull a muscle, I need to rest my body. The world, our world, is one organism. The planet is one being. Just because something is happening 10,000 miles away from us doesn't mean it doesn't systemically have an impact on us. It does. And that's why each of us has to take responsibility for our own healing, authenticity, self-expression, and inner power.

☉

This book represents the beginning of a new chapter in my life. I have healed my life in some areas, but my healing is a lifelong journey. New moments in time reveal opportunities to heal in newer, deeper ways, and so my story, my journey, continues.

I could write a book about writing my book, seriously. I went through so many battles, iterations, both internally and externally. From a "Go ahead and write your book, it's your story," to "Who do you think you are, writing your whole story?" to "My blessings are with you," to "STOP RIGHT NOW!!"

I even had a version of this book in which I changed the identity of my father to a "friend of the family." Reading that version over made me want to throw up, I was so disgusted. Here I was, wanting to tell my story so I could speak the unspeakable, but instead, I spent my energy coming up with a whole new version of my life just so that my book would land gently for a handful of people. In doing so I was completely failing to fulfill the very purpose of the book—to offer hope and guidance to those still held back by their denial of their past, older versions of themselves.

I reverted to my work on this, the original version of the book, and was well along with a few rounds of edits when I found out that I was not the only one my father had abused. On a trip to my cousin's home in California, I discovered that the reason we were separated for such a long time was because my father had not only had an affair with her mother, but had made inappropriate advances toward her as well. Although nothing happened between them, I was deeply disturbed by this revelation and felt betrayed at a new level. I felt like all the healing and the trust that had taken so many years and tears to rebuild were all a lie, a waste of my life. I felt cheated. When confronted, my father admitted this to me, saying that the other relationships were not like the one he had with me. I am unsure how to react to that statement, even now.

Every year since the beginning of my writing this book, I have had a dream about my father on Father's Day. The first dream occurred in 2012. I woke up startled. In the dream, my father had just died, but rather than grieving, I am panicking, asking questions like, *What did we not complete in our relationship? What did we not say to each other?* Was this dream a premonition? I don't know.

The following year came the death of two of my uncles, Ravi Baswani and Mitran Devanesan, both of whom I loved dearly and to whom I was very close. They were like fathers to me, mentors and friends. Their loss was very painful. That year again I had a dream on Father's Day. The dream featured a deceased version of my father and my actually deceased uncles, and we were at a funeral for all three of them. Again I am wondering in the dream, *How could my father die? He was healthy, practiced yoga daily, ran over a dozen marathons.* The questions I asked myself were clinical, unemotional; I was not distressed, just puzzled.

The third year, in 2014, before I had learned about my father's attempted abuse of my cousin, I dreamed of his death again. This time the dream brought with it what I interpreted as answers. In this latest dream, I learned that my father succumbed to a heart attack. And again, I had questions. *But his heart was healthy; he just had a full physical checkup and everything was fine. How then could this have happened?* Again, I was not sentimental or upset. And then the answer came to me: *He did not die of an unhealthy heart, he died of a broken heart.*

By this third dream, since I had not yet been to see my cousin in California, I couldn't know what the months following that visit would unravel, so that now, today, my aged father is alone. My mother has left him, finally forging her own path and finding her place in this world independently. My father has lost his house, the roof over his head, and his business. He has no retirement or assets that I know of. He does not have his wife, children, or grandchildren beside him.

At a cost of not caring what I needed in terms of safe space and help, my old self would have wanted to immediately make things better—harmonious—by doing whatever was necessary to look like a "normal" family, urge everyone to get along, be just like my mother in wondering why we couldn't all be one big, happy family.

But not this time. This time, it's different. Maybe I have grown up, and while I am still fiercely optimistic and believing in possibilities, I have learned to love, respect, and honor myself. No one is going to if I don't. I still have abundant love and compassion for my father, and I want peace, healing, and forgiveness for him. It would be great if our paths cross again, in time. For now, I believe the time and space between us is healing me in many new ways, unlike before. It is helping me be grounded and self-aware as I complete the writing of this book—probably the scariest thing I have ever attempted to do in my life.

This time, I guess, I have been asking myself, *Why didn't my father come clean with me once and for all when we sat in the orchid garden? We had an opportunity then to be complete, not hold back. How could this be happening right now?*

But the truth is that this *is* happening, and nothing can be done to change this reality except embrace it. When I first learned about my California cousin, of course I went through myriad emotions: I felt like a fraud—that everything I had taught, what I had said to my students, all of it was a lie. I felt I had no authority or credibility to be who I say I am. And then it dawned on me that, despite this new turn of events, my healing journey of the past, what I had accomplished and achieved in my life—none of that was fake. All this is as real as it gets. If anything, putting my own methods to the test only made me stronger and clearer about how my practices work.

After this second breakup with my father, I discovered that I still had compassion for him. I truly hope he finds peace. Previously, my forgiveness included an unconditional reconciliation in which we all became a happy family again. The truth is that while that sounds like an idyllic development, it is not what feels natural right now, and I am OK with that. My father and I have had plenty of karmic and energetic exchanges in this lifetime. Right now it is time for both of us to find peace. My father's last email to me summed it up pretty well:

Dear Richa:

I have been trying to figure out our past. The only thing I understand is that I offer unconditional apologies to all those who have been wronged by me knowingly or unknowingly. It is an enormous task to face up to the consequences of your actions. But there is NO escape any way. To face the challenge with humility seems the only solution.

Whatever be the philosophy—one needs one's own near and dear ones to face life. Ultimately it is family, which can make or break a person. One would have wished that I were the anchor giving the support and stability. But life is what is happening NOW.

My sincere prayer is that one day we would all be together and be able to share our life. It is extremely precious and not to be lost. Even a brief moment is not to be given to despair. I keep telling myself that I should be positive and move forward but I do succumb to low times and remain there for ages. My wife had been the support I could turn to in my difficult times. How I wish not to lose her.

You all mean the world to me and without all of you this whole beautiful world has no attraction. I love you all and shall always—forever.

Do forgive me and give me a small place in your heart.

Papa

7

A Letter to My Daughters

A Letter to My Daughters

July 20, 2012

Dear Ananya, Rena, and Aishwarya,

This is Mommy. So now you know what happened to Mommy
as a young girl. You know how it happened, who did what,
and how Mommy handled her life.

As you know, growing up is a lot of work! It was for Mommy too. With a few extra twists and turns along the way. Even
though it seemed like a lot to handle when I was a little girl, I
think I managed myself quite well.

Today, I look at the wonderful young women the three of
you are growing up to be. I am so happy that I was able to overcome the hurdles in my younger days. It helped me be a better
mother. It helped me step back from my own stories so I could
celebrate the magnificence of your lives.

They say that babies choose their parents. Thank you for
choosing me to be your mother in this lifetime. Thank you
for giving me the honor to be a witness to your journey and

for letting me be a part of it. Most of all, thank you for healing me, your Mommy.

I know it was no accident that Daddy and I were blessed with not just one but three daughters. We feel most blessed that we have you, our own "Three Goddesses." The three of you came into our life to give us three times the love.

I know there may have been times that I was overprotective of you. I didn't want anything to go wrong in your life. I didn't want to fail as your mother. Please forgive me if you felt like I denied you your space. It was not my intention. I only had your best interest at heart. I was still healing and learning that it was OK to let go. It might have taken a little longer at times. So I hope you will forgive me.

I want you to live your life to your fullest potential. I want you to trust, love, and thrive in your lives. Above all I want you to trust your instincts, trust your gut, and celebrate who you are, because you all are wonderful. If anyone says otherwise, ask them to talk to Daddy.

I hope you all know how much Mommy loves you. You three are the reason I decided to write this book so other mommies, daddies, and grownups would know that even though something terrible might have happened to them as a child, there is still hope. I hope you three will help other children who may be in the kind of trouble Mommy was in when she was little. These children need friends who can listen to them without thinking of them as bad kids.

When kids learn more about their personal safety, they can take care of themselves. They don't get into trouble like Mommy did. Wouldn't it be great if we could stop this from happening to other kids? I think it would be worth it, don't you?

But this is your life and this is your choice. You don't have to do anything because Mommy is asking you to. You should do whatever you feel like doing, and I will be there to support you. Even if it's becoming a hairdresser who is a farmer who does fashion in the evenings and is a doctor on the weekends. That's who you, Ananya, said you wanted to be when you grew up. You were six.

This book is dedicated to the three of you, my three little angels, my three goddesses, my three wishes that came true. You have healed me immeasurably. I dedicate this book to you and your generation of friends—brothers and sisters who might be looking for a way to heal. Your generation will become mommies and daddies too one day. My dream is that the ripples of the thoughts contained in these pages will help in healing others for many years to come.

With all my love and blessings,

Always your one and only,

Mommy

Xoxox

Acknowledgments

There are several people without whom this book may never have been written. I remember the day I shared the story of my past with Dr. Rama, our family homeopath. I had gone to see her for an assortment of skin allergies I had at the time. By then I had learned that my emotional and mental state played a role in my physical health. This was right after I had realized that my marriage to Sid was at a dead end and had just about had my first retreat experience with Prema. In confidence, I decided to tell Dr. Rama, who knew my parents well. The first words out of her mouth were, "You should write a book," an idea I immediately dismissed.

"No, I will never do that, there is no way."

Despite my spontaneous refusal, a seed was planted that lay dormant for the following 15 years of my life. It was while I was leading my retreats that my team and participants started to ask deeper questions, wanting to know me, about how I started in this work.

Some assumed I was already in the process of writing a book and would be surprised to discover a contradicting response from me.

"So, you are writing a book, yes?"

"When will your book come out?"

"You know, if you just had a book . . . !"

Hence, I owe it to my dearest team from that very first day of my first retreat, my friends and sisters, Nicol Pomeroy, Mina Fies, and Dawn Coleman, for putting up with my intensity and my seemingly unreasonable demands. You all made every retreat experience what it was—and they were powerful, transformative, and incredibly fun, despite the tears and primal screaming! Even when the way up the hill to Kayser Ridge was packed with 18 inches of ice, we still made it! As a team, we have, together, caused transformation for more than a hundred beings on this planet. Isn't that amazing? Thank you for leading beside me, having my back, and making our retreats the one-of-a-kind, life-changing weekends they have been and continue to be.

Once I made my decision that I was going to write my book, I asked my student, Reina Weiner, speaker and author of *Strong from the Start* and the upcoming *Trust Your Doctor, but Not Too Much*, to be my book-writing coach. In the initial phase of this work, Reina's support and direct, New York style of just saying it as she saw it was incredible for me. I started a Word document with Reina-isms like, "If you feel like writing, write. If you don't feel like writing, write." I thank her for her patience at a time I had so many questions and unknowns. And I thank her for helping me find the clarity I needed at a very vulnerable time.

A few years ago I met four-time Emmy Award–winner Jan Fox to discuss my work as a professional speaker. I gave her the context of my book and I will never forget what she said.

"In all my years of reporting on every imaginable story there could be, from war, to burglary, sexual assault, and entertaining events, I have never come across a story like yours. I can't wait to read your book and help you share it on the world stage."

For so long I had held the belief that my story was just what happened to me many years ago. I would help people along the way and carry on. But when I heard these words from Jan, I could see that I had my work cut out for me. I felt it deep in my bones that day; there was no looking the other way. I was going to complete this journey.

After a year and a half of writing and then setting my book aside, my path crossed with Steve Dorfman's. I had met Steve many times and he came to mind as someone I might want to interview for my *Pause For Power* TV and radio show, and so I did. Right after my event, he unexpectedly turned around and asked if he could interview me on his show, called *We Mean Business TV*, and help bring *Pause for Power* to his viewers. And so we did that. After the filming of this interview, we went to lunch where Steve explained that he was writing a book as well. We found that we had a lot in common and decided to become each other's book-writing accountability partners. And thus began our journey of a friendship that will last a lifetime. Steve and I spent three hours every week either in person or over Skype, and he would write his book, and I mine. We would check in with each other, help brainstorm, get out of our own way, and keep the flow going. During this process, which lasted over a year, I went through ups and downs. There are no words, but I will try to thank Steve for his unconditional love and support and for holding a space for me to heal as I wrote. He handed me the Kleenex and brought me water as I cried when the sad feelings would come up while writing. He laughed with me when I was being goofy and joking. Steve, you are a true friend, and this book would not be here without your being on this journey with me.

One of my closest friends and soul sisters on the planet, Lisa Messano, a "bloody good writer" as I once lovingly called her, has been by my side throughout the process of writing *Coming Home to the Heart*. From scraping me off the ground when I would crash from the pain of writing about my experience, to celebrating the completion of each little chapter, to finalizing the title of the book—she has truly been a soul companion on my journey of this book and of my life. There is nothing I have not shared with Lisa, and acknowledging or thanking her seems weak and dry compared to the intense gratitude I feel for the gift of her just being in my life.

One of the many wonderful things that came out of my initial work with Reina Weiner was that she introduced me to my editor, Kathy Hollen. Because Kathy now only works on select projects, I thought I won the lottery when she agreed to work with me. Perhaps it was her no-nonsense attitude while still being compassionate and funny that really made me feel like we would make a good team. I remember the knots I would feel in my stomach every time I received an email from her. I would be excited yet so nervous. Being highly experienced and excellent at what she does, she would get straight to the point. She did not mince her words but always knew how to close with very gentle and kind remarks. This being the emotional roller coaster that it had been for me, I thank her for staying and not jumping off the ride, especially when it would sometimes take me months to respond to her emails. She asked me so many questions, many of which I never wanted to answer. But then, in the end, I did. For sure, I would not have if Kathy had not been my editor.

I thank Craig Hines for the beautiful design of my book cover as well as the interior layout. I thank Laura d'All with Copy General for the printing and online fulfillment of *Coming Home to the Heart* and Charles Martin for my photograph on the cover of this book.

My thanks and gratitude would not be complete if I didn't thank my rock, my pillar of strength, my one and only—for better or for worse, my darling husband, Kash. He has been hearing me incessantly repeat for the past several years, "I really need to finish my book." And now, honey, here we are! Let the next chapter of the journey begin.

I thank my three little angels, my three little goddesses, my daughters Ananya, Rena, and Aishwarya. You make me smile and sometimes cry with the pangs of a love so deep for you that I feel in every fiber of my being. You have shown me the true face of happiness in your own. This love is like no other, and I feel so lucky to experience it—thanks to you.

I thank my older brother, Sourabh; his wife, Sapna; and my younger brother, Suhaas, for their unconditional love and support of me on this journey. I thank my friends who have contributed to my journey of healing at various stages and ages of my life—Meghna, Vini, Parag, Uday, Dr. Ratna, Aarti, Aditi, Raju, Vasu, Bhuvana, Anand and Mali.

I thank my teachers and coaches from all over the world, Prema (transformation, Reiki, retreats), Dr. Usui (founder of Reiki), Dr. Paula Horan (bodywork), Narayan (Medicine Buddha Reiki), Dr. Balakumar (feng shui, Bach flowers), Mr. Ebrahim Alkazi (theater), Malathi Rangarajan (English), Ganga Krishnan (school headmistress), Ms. Gowri (mantra chanting), and Sister Edwina (piano).

I thank my parents for bringing me into this world so that I could have all the experiences I have had in my life. I would not be here right now, finishing *Coming Home to the Heart*, having the life I have, being on this journey of transformation and healing the way I am if my parents had not been exactly who they are. I thank you for teaching me so much in this lifetime and being OK with the revelations made in this book. I acknowledge you for bringing me into this life and truly setting me free to follow my path.

Above all I thank, acknowledge, and pay homage to the divine spirit that is omnipresent, omniscient, and all-encompassing for breathing through me the life force I needed to see *Coming Home to the Heart* through—figuratively holding my hand to "bring it home." Without this divine grace, I don't believe my fingers could have ever typed a single word. Left to me, this book may never have been written. At every stage of my life, from childhood through motherhood, I know this divine love has always been with me, within me, calling me forth to be with it in stillness. I thank this grace, and, deeply bowing, offer myself to the work of this divine intelligence that continues to invisibly yet so powerfully show me the way on my journey. When I feel lost, you bring me the sign I need to make the right turn. When I feel alone, you send me exactly whom I need to meet in my life. I know you are here; your presence in me and around me is strong. When I forget about you, you patiently await my return to come home to you. And when I do, you ground me, you center me, you balance me, you unconditionally love me. Dear divine light, you who lead me, all you beings who guide me, I honor you. I thank you. I acknowledge you. I AM because you are in my life. You are why I am *Coming Home to the Heart*. Namaste!

Suggested Reading

Bach, Richard. *Jonathan Livingston Seagull: A Story*. New York: Scribner, 1970.

Brennan, Barbara Ann. *Hands of Light: A Guide to Healing through the Human Energy Field*. New York: Bantam, 1987.

Chopra, Deepak. *Ageless Body, Timeless Mind: The Quantum Alternative to Growing Old*. New York: Harmony Books, 1993.

Chopra, Deepak. *The Path to Love: Spiritual Lessons for Creating the Love You Need*. New York: Harmony Books, 1997.

A Course in Miracles. Combined vol. 3rd ed., including text, teacher's manual, workbook. Mill Valley: Foundation for Inner Peace, 2007.

Courtois, Christine. *Healing the Incest Wound: Adult Survivors in Therapy*. New York: W. W. Norton & Company, 1988.

Ehrmann, Max. "Desiderata." *The Poems of Max Ehrmann*. Boston: Bruce Humphries Publishing Company, 1948.

Goldstein, Jim. *Powerful Partnerships: The Power to Transform Any Relationship into a Great One!* www.jimgoldstein.com, 2010.

Hay, Louise L. *You Can Heal Your Life*. Santa Monica: Hay House, 1982.

His Holiness the Dalai Lama. *Ethics for the New Millenium*. New York: Riverhead Books, 1999.

Lübeck, Walter, Frank Arjava Petter, and William Lee Rand. *The Spirit of Reiki: The Complete Handbook of the Reiki System*. Twin Lakes: Lotus Press / Shangri-La, 2001.

Myss, Caroline. *Anatomy of the Spirit: The Seven Stages of Power and Healing*. New York: Three Rivers Press, 1996.

Osho. *The Book of Secrets*. New York: St. Martin's Griffin, 1974.

Parkyn, Chetan. *Human Design: Discover the Person You Were Born to Be*. Novato: New World Library, 2009.

Pirsig, Robert M. *Zen and the Art of Motorcycle Maintenance: An Inquiry into Values*. New York: Harper Torch, 1974.

Rilke, Rainer Maria (M. D. Herter Norton, trans.). *Letters to a Young Poet*. New York: W. W. Norton & Co., 1934.

Tsabary, Shefali. *The Conscious Parent: Transforming Ourselves, Empowering Our Children*. Vancouver: Namaste Publishing, 2010.

Vasudevan, Bhanumathy. *Psychic Moon: Channeled Teaching to Women of This Century*. Bangalore: W. Q. Judge Press, 2010.

Yeshe, Lama. *Medicine Dharma Reiki: An Introduction to the Secret Inner Practices*. New Delhi: Full Circle, 2001.

Yogananda, Paramahansa. *The Autobiography of a Yogi*. New York: Philosophical Library, 1946.

86451095R00090

Made in the USA
Columbia, SC
15 January 2018